The Ethics of Employment Screening for Psychopathy

The Ethics of Employment Screening for Psychopathy

Brian K. Steverson

LEXINGTON BOOKS
Lanham • Boulder • New York • London

Published by Lexington Books
An imprint of The Rowman & Littlefield Publishing Group, Inc.
4501 Forbes Boulevard, Suite 200, Lanham, Maryland 20706
www.rowman.com

6 Tinworth Street, London SE11 5AL, United Kingdom

British Library Cataloguing in Publication Information Available

Library of Congress Cataloging-in-Publication Data

Names: Steverson, Brian K., 1961- author.
Title: The ethics of employment screening for psychopathy / Brian K. Steverson.
Description: Lanham : Lexington Books, 2020. | Includes bibliographical references and index. | Summary: "This book argues that, despite recent calls to arms to seek out and remove "corporate psychopaths" from the business world, efforts to eliminate the corporate psychopath presence would be illegal as well as unethical"—Provided by publisher.
Identifiers: LCCN 2020029981 (print) | LCCN 2020029982 (ebook) | ISBN 9781793616821 (cloth) | ISBN 9781793616838 (epub)
Subjects: LCSH: United States. Americans with Disabilities Act of 1990. | Employee screening—Moral and ethical aspects—United States. | Psychopaths—Employment—Moral and ethical aspects—United States. | Psychology, Industrial—United States. | Psychopaths—Legal status, laws, etc.—United States. | Business ethics—United States.
Classification: LCC HF5549.5.E429 S63 2020 (print) | LCC HF5549.5.E429 (ebook) | DDC 174/.4—dc23
LC record available at https://lccn.loc.gov/2020029981
LC ebook record available at https://lccn.loc.gov/2020029982

Contents

Introduction

Silence of The Lambs hit movie theatres in 1991, sparking an almost three-decade-long public fascination with psychopaths. Dozens of books on psychopaths and their "life among us" have appeared in the popular press over that time, including the following:

- *Without Conscience: The Disturbing World of the Psychopaths Among Us* (Robert Hare, 1993)
- *Working With Monsters: How to Identify and Protect Yourself From the Workplace Psychopath* (John Clarke, 2005).
- *Snakes in Suits: When Psychopaths Go to Work* (Paul Babiak & Robert Hare, 2006)
- *The Psychopath Test: A Journey Through the Madness Industry* (Jon Ronson, 2011).
- *The Wisdom of Psychopaths: What Saints, Spies, and Serial Killers Can Teach Us About Success* (Kevin Dutton, 2012)
- *The Psychopath Inside: A Neuroscientist's Journey Into the Dark Side of the Brain* (James Fallon, 2013)
- *The Psychopath Whisperer: The Science of Those Without Conscience* (Kent Kiehl, 2014)

Clarke has even published a compact "guide" filled with tips and tricks for protecting oneself against the workplace psychopath, *The Pocket Psycho* (Clarke, 2007). The tally of popular publications on the subject easily doubles if one includes "sociopaths" as a close cousin to "psychopaths." The portrayal of fictional psychopathic characters in popular movies has even been studied academically (Leistedt & Linkowski, 2014).

Similarly, academic interest in psychopathy mushroomed during this time (a quick Google Scholar search shows around 44,000 entries for publications with "psychopathy" in the title for the 1990–2018 time period). In the field of business ethics itself, the last few decades have witnessed a flurry of activity aimed at establishing a worrisome concern for the presence of psychopaths in the workplace, particularly in higher-level management and even more particularly in the corporate world (a quick search of the top two journals in the field, *Journal of Business Ethics* and *Business Ethics Quarterly*, shows that around 60 articles directly or indirectly addressing psychopathy in the workplace have appeared). A distinct label for psychopaths functioning in big business, "corporate psychopaths," has even emerged in the literature.

To this point, academic discussion of corporate psychopaths has focused on establishing their presence, developing the means by which to identify them, documenting the intraorganizational and economic harm they cause, and calling for their ouster from the workplace. Clive Boddy, Paul Babiak, and Robert Hare have gathered evidence over the past twenty-five years that indicates that 3%–5% of managers and senior-level positions in the corporate setting are held by psychopaths, compared to a presence of only 1% from the general population. Recognizing the difficulty involved in gathering large data sets on the matter, corporations have any number of reasons for denying psychopathy researchers access to their employees for testing; the data that has been gathered is alarming in what it reveals about the potential for psychopaths in the workplace to wreak havoc on the well-being of those around them, on the health of the organizations they inhabit, and on the larger economic and social systems in which those organizations are embedded. The presence of corporate psychopaths has even been described as "perhaps the most significant threat to ethical corporate behavior around the world" (Marshall et al., 2014, p. 495). Unsurprisingly, a "call to arms" (Boddy's phrase) has been issued to "weed out" psychopathic persons from the workplace. Citing his own research in support of the Corporate Psychopath Hypothesis, to be presented in chapter two, Boddy remarks that "[t]he arguments around the calls for the screening of Corporate Psychopaths in senior positions within corporations are thereby strengthened," and, due to the enhanced opportunities to be "organizational destroyers" presented by their positions of power, "it is logical to propose that the higher the position that is to be filled by the new recruitment, the more beneficial it would be to screen job applicants for psychopathy" (Boddy, 2014, p. 118). It has even been suggested that HR professionals within organizations adopt, metaphorically at least, the anti-terrorist, military strategy of "seek and destroy" in their efforts to identify and eliminate corporate psychopaths from the workplace (Marshal et al., 2014).

What has yet to be addressed in the academic discussion is a consideration of the ethical issues that might attach to attempts to eliminate or minimize the presence of corporate psychopaths. Clarke recognized this gap in the discussion of the phenomenon of corporate psychopaths as far back as 2005:

> From a legislative perspective, each company has a duty of care to their employees to ensure that no personal harm is caused them as a result of their work. In theory this precludes an organizational psychopath being employed in many cases. In practice, companies do not deliberately employ the organizational psychopath. Therefore the question must be asked, should companies be doing more to detect organizational psychopaths entering their organization, and should they implement policies that increase the probability of such psychopaths being detected and managed once they are working in an organization. One final, but very important question concerns the rights of the organizational psychopath themselves. How does one achieve a balance between the rights of the psychopath and the rights of their victims not to be victimized? Is it discrimination to sack an employee solely on the grounds of having a personality disorder such as psychopathy? All of these questions must be answered before a solution to the issue of psychopaths in the workplace can be resolved. (Clarke, 2005, p. 171)

In his academic monograph, *Corporate Psychopaths: Organisational Destroyers*, one of only a few books to address the issue of psychopaths in the workplace, Boddy devotes only one page to the ethical issues that might attend employment psychopathy screening, and he only notes that there are ethical issues with identifying psychopaths in the workplace without mentioning what they might be. In another book, *Snakes in Suits: When Psychopaths Go to Work*, Babiak and Hare make no mention of the matter. This text is intended to fill that glaring omission, and, in that way, would be the first of its kind. Counterintuitive as it might sound, given the public image of psychopaths, testing for psychopathy, both as part of the pre-employment screening process and as part of regular reviews of employees, may be both illegal, per the Americans with Disabilities Act, and run afoul of some basic principles of just treatment. In defense of that conclusion, this work attempts to answer questions such as,

- Is psychopathy a covered disability under the ADA?
- If so, are employers obligated to provide accommodations for employees with psychopathic personalities?
- Does pre-employment screening of job applicants for psychopathy run the risk of denying some applicants equal opportunity?
- Does screening for psychopathy cause unjustified harm to applicants and employees?

- Does screening for psychopathy in the employment arena constitute an unnecessary privacy violation?

The general conclusion of this work is that psychopathy would qualify as an ADA-covered disability, and because of that, employers would only be able to test for it under restricted circumstances. Also, employers may indeed be required to provide reasonable workplace accommodations for individuals labeled "functioning psychopaths." Apart from legal considerations, it will be argued that screening for psychopathy, partly due to some standing questions about the reliability and predictive validity of the diagnostic instruments that would likely be involved in any screening practice, would indeed violate some important principles of just treatment of human beings, and, hence, would be unethical even if the legal case against screening for psychopathy were to change.

It has not been *argued* directly that psychopathy screens like the PCL-R, the PCL:SV, the B-Scan, or the PM-MRV be used as part of corporate hiring processes, as part of individual performance reviews, or as part of organization-wide employee review initiatives, though Boddy does mention in passing that "eventually" a screening tool like the B-Scan could be used "as part of the usual batch of intelligence and personality tests carried out by human resources departments" to screen for the presence of psychopathic personalities in the hiring process (Boddy, 2005, p. 37). Nevertheless if calls for the removal of psychopathic personalities from the workplace are to be taken seriously and an employer could have at their disposal a psychiatric screening tool like the B-Scan or the PM-MRV designed to be used in an organizational setting (as opposed to ones designed to be used in clinical and forensic settings), then it is natural to conclude that efforts to minimize the danger corporate psychopaths pose *should* include pre-employment and post-hire screening using one or more of these screening tools. Other methods for weeding out corporate psychopaths have been directly promoted, mostly for use during the hiring process, such as thorough verification of resume information and training of interviewers to be on the alert for inconsistencies in interviewee responses. Marshall et al., (2014) are confident that if given the requisite intraorganizational power to do so, human resources management would be able to identify and remove corporate psychopaths from the workplace.

> There is an obvious and important opportunity for HRM professions to improve their corporate performance by developing strategies towards eliminating CP. The plain need to combat CP can give ambitious HRM professionals strong arguments for increasing their status and influence within conceivably any large organization. Specifically, the profession can argue that if given adequate boardroom sanction and support to scrutinize and performance appraise man-

> agement at the highest levels, and if permitted to harness its traditional resources to steer or redesign organizational culture—including the cultural "tone at the top"—then HRM strategies so empowered may finally be able to reduce CP at all organizational levels. (Marshall et al., 2014, p. 496).

Though human resources professionals may be better trained at using these indirect methods for identifying psychopathic personalities than they would be with psychiatric screens like the PCL-R, there is the question of how effective these traditional screens would be in actually identifying psychopathic personalities. Given that psychopathic persons are adept at "hiding" themselves from detection, it is reasonable to believe they would be able to pass unnoticed through traditional hiring practices like interviews, letters of reference, and background checks. If the data on the presence of corporate psychopaths presented in chapter two is accurate, then these psychopathic personalities have already been remarkably adept at avoiding detection during hiring and review processes. Consequently, if efforts to remove the psychopathic presence from the workplace are to be executed most effectively, they ought to include psychiatric screening for psychopathic personalities.

There are a few stylistic practices to be used in this text that need some explanation. First, except where the term is used by cited authors and in quotes, "psychopath" will not be used to refer to the individuals considered to be corporate psychopaths. Instead, we will use the term "psychopathic personalities" in reference to those individuals. As will be discussed in chapter one, psychopathy is not a categorical construct, but a dimensional one. There does not exist a very thick and easily discernable line between individuals who would qualify as psychopathic and those who would not. The type of screening used to reach a diagnosis of psychopathy involves interpretation on the part of the clinician administering the screening. As will be discussed in chapter four, there have always been concerns about the interrater reliability of the screening instruments used. Psychopathy is not itself a personality trait that one either has or does not have, as would be the case if it were a categorical psychological construct. Instead it is present when a constellation of underlying personality traits are present in a dominant fashion. Put roughly, each of us possesses some of the traits constitutive of psychopathy to some degree. This is what makes it a dimensional psychological construct. Labeling individuals as "psychopaths" has the tendency to create the impression that psychopathy is categorical in nature. Using the phrasing "psychopathic personality," we believe, has less of a tendency to do that inasmuch as the reference is directly to the personality and not the individual, and because it allows that some personalities can be more psychopath*ic* than others. This is an important consideration to keep in mind when it comes time to talk about the ethical issues surrounding employment screening for psychopathy, as we will do in chapter four, because if deployed systematically and driven by employer interests, it is quite likely that screeners will be asked by employers to "err on the side of caution" and designate as "undesirable" individuals whose screening score would not qualify them as psychopathic in clinical or forensic settings.

A second stylistic adoption for this text is the use of a reference to the corporate psychopath phenomenon discussed in the academic literature, including the call to remove them from the workplace, as the Corporate Psychopath Hypothesis. It will be capitalized so as to be consistent with a style adopted by Boddy, who more than any other researcher and author has written about psychopaths in the ranks of corporate managers and executives, and by others working in the area. The content of the Corporate Psychopath Hypothesis will be explained in chapter two. "Corporate Psychopath" will be used generally to refer to any psychopathic personality occupying a managerial or senior-level position in a business organization, whether or not the organization is a publicly traded corporation.

Chapter one will open with a presentation of the history of "psychopathy" as a construct in the study of human psychology. As we will see, though the reference to "psychopaths" first appeared in the late nineteenth century, psychologists and other students of human nature, for example philosophers, have described types of individuals possessed of personality traits that would qualify them for diagnoses as "psychopaths" in modern psychological studies. An account of the modern conception of "psychopathy" will follow, including descriptions of the most widely used psychopathy screening instruments like the PCL-R. Throughout its history, the Diagnostic and Statistical Manual (the DSM), the authoritative guide for the diagnosis of mental disorders, has failed to list "psychopathy" as a distinct mental disorder. The fundamental disagreement over that ongoing decision will be discussed, as that debate illuminates some of the features of "psychopathy" as a mental disorder, which are crucial to the arguments composing the Corporate Psychopath Hypothesis.

Chapter two takes up the Corporate Psychopath Hypothesis directly. The Corporate Psychopath Hypothesis has an empirical part and a normative part. The empirical part, the research supporting claims about the size of the presence of Corporate Psychopaths and the research linking that presence to a range of harms to coworkers, organizations themselves, and the larger social/economic systems in which Corporate Psychopaths operate will be presented in detail, as this forms the foundation for the normative calls to "seek and destroy" them. Those normative arguments will be laid out in detail as well. The quality of the empirical research and the normative arguments will not itself be critically assessed in this chapter, though it will be in later chapters to some extent. The purpose of this text is not to critically engage with the entirety of the Corporate Psychopath Hypothesis, but rather to fill in a gap in the hypothesis regarding the ethics of heeding the calls to "seek and destroy" Corporate Psychopaths.

Chapter three examines the relationship between the Americans with Disabilities Act and a diagnosis of psychopathy. The crux of the relationship is whether or not psychopathy would qualify as a covered disability under the ADA. If it does, or it could be argued that it should be covered, then general employment psychopathy screening, both during the hiring process and as part of employee performance reviews, would likely be illegal. Pinning down which bodily or psychological conditions would qualify as "disabilities" under the ADA requires some interpretive work, especially regarding mental disorders. The matter of ADA-required accommodations for psychopathic personalities in the workplace will also be discussed.

As counterintuitive as it sounds, chapter four presents the argument that, apart from its legal status, employment psychopathy screening would in almost all cases be unethical. Issues concerning equal opportunity, job applicant and employee rights to privacy, and utilitarian considerations form the arguments to support the broad conclusion that employment psychopathy screening violates some foundational ethical and justice commitments that we recognize as operative in the world of employment.

The concluding chapter sums up the intent and arguments of this text, while also casting an eye toward further questions to explore regarding the serious issues presented in the Corporate Psychopath Hypothesis. As will be noted, the Corporate Psychopath Hypothesis raises very serious concerns about the well-being of non-psychopathic employees and the health of organizations where psychopathic persons might work. It is not the intent of this text to dismiss those concerns. They deserve the attention not just of researchers but also of those employers whose business organizations might present a safe haven for Corporate Psychopaths. How to proceed to address those concerns and mitigate the organizational risks presented by Corporate Psychopaths in an ethical and legal way is what remains to be worked out. Some suggestions on how to proceed will be offered.

Chapter One

Psychopathy Defined

THE HISTORY OF PSYCHOPATHY

The modern construct of "psychopathy" has only been around since the mid-20th century, though the identification of some of the personality traits central to the modern understanding of psychopathy dates back at least as far as the early 1800s. This is not to say that observers of human nature were unaware of the personality type currently labelled "psychopathic" centuries before that. Theophrastus, a student of Aristotle, commented on a group of individuals who seemed to fail to be capable of forming those interpersonal relationships that typically bind members of communities that he called "the unscrupulous." Retrospective judgments about psychopathic personalities are often made. Kiehl and Hoffman, for example state the following:

> Psychopathy has always been part of human society; that is evident from its ubiquity in history's myths and literature. Greek and Roman mythology is strewn with psychopaths, Medea being the most obvious. Psychopaths populate the Bible, at least the Old Testament, perhaps beginning with Cain. Psychopaths have appeared in a steady stream of literature from all cultures since humans first put pen to paper: from King Shahyar in *The Book of One Thousand and One Nights*; to the psychopaths in Shakespeare, including Richard III and, perhaps most chillingly, Aaron the Moor in *Titus Andronicus*; to the villain Ximen Qing in the 17th century Chinese epic *Jin Ping Mei*, The Golden Vase. (Kiehl & Hoffman, 2011, p. 359)

The French doctor, Phillipe Pinel, who is often cited in the literature as the founding father of modern psychiatry, is credited with describing a group of patients who were intellectually sound, but nonetheless exhibited characteristics like cruelty, antisocial behavior, irresponsibility, and immorality at the beginning of the 19th century. He called this personality type *mania sans delire* (insanity without delirium). Though not a direct equivalent to the modern construct of "psychopathy," Pinel's categorization of individuals possessing these personality traits as being psychologically disordered presages contemporary work in the study of psychopathy. Pinel identified that some of his patients, though they were entirely capable of comprehending the immorality of their behavior, were prone to impulsive acts of extreme violence and self-harm. They did not seem to suffer from what we would now call psychoses, hence the label "insanity without delirium" (Arrigo & Shipley, 2001).

J. C. Prichard, the first to use the expression "moral insanity," described the condition as "a morbid perversion of the natural feelings, affections, inclinations, temper, habits, moral dispositions, and natural impulses, without any remarkable disorder or defect of the intellect or knowing and reasoning faculties, and particularly without any insane illusion or hallucination" (Arrigo & Shipley, 2001, pp. 330–331). A broad category of mental disorder, Prichard's "moral insanity" would include under its descriptive umbrella a number of disorders recognized by modern psychology as distinctive. The classification, for Prichard, also carried with it moral condemnation, a state of being deserving of social approbation. He postulated that those individuals possessed with "moral insanity" were not amoral, incapable of distinguishing between right and wrong, they simply suffered from an inability to willfully resist the impulses they felt.

The term "psychopath" owes its origin to the work of the German psychiatrist J. L. A. Koch, who coined the term "psychopastiche" (literally, "suffering soul") in 1888 (Koch, 1888). He published a second text over a three year period, 1891–1893, Die psychopathischen Minderwertigkeiten *(Psychopathic Inferiority)*, in which he distinguished "psychopathic inferiority" from other types of psychopathologies. He ordered psychopathologies into two forms, congenital and acquired, each with differing levels of severity, and attempted to develop a *gestalt* approach to diagnosing psychopathic inferiority that made for a more comprehensive treatment of the disorder. For the congenital form, Koch divided it into three groups: (a) psychopathic disposition—psychic tenderness in an asthenic individual; (b) psychic inferiority—vulnerable types (sensitive and weak), vigorous types (grandiose, troublemaker), and the intermediate types (blunted nature); and (c) psychopathic degeneration—intellectual and moral failure caused by cerebral defects (Arrigo & Shipley, 2001, pp. 331–332). However, as Kiehl and Hoffman explain,

> . . . in exchange for more theoretical diagnostic clarity, the so called German School of psychopathy expanded the diagnosis to include people who hurt themselves as well as others, and in the process seemed to lose sight of the moral disability that was at the core of the condition. By the time of the Great

> Depression, psychiatry was using the word psychopath to include people who were depressed, weak-willed, excessively shy and insecure—in other words, almost anyone deemed abnormal. The true psychopath had, once again, become academically, if not clinically, hidden. (2011, p. 364).

For the first few decades of the 1900s, "psychopathy" was a widely used label to apply to any subject deemed to have an abnormal psychology. One notable exception was Emil Kraepelin, who worked to restrict the overly broad use of "psychopathic" to just those individuals who displayed the most destructive traits. He broke down the psychopathic category into four types: (a) born criminals, (b) pathological liars, (c) professional criminals who acted out of calculated self-interest rather than impulse, and (d) individuals "who wandered through life with neither self-confidence nor responsibility" (Arrigo & Shipley, 2001, p. 333). A major and permanent shift away from the catch-all usage of "psychopathy" began in 1939 and 1941 with the publication of two texts that would establish the basis for the modern construct of "psychopathy" by identifying the core affective personality traits that are at the heart of the attribution of a psychopathic personality, thereby offering the possibility of more diagnostic precision. In 1939, Scottish psychiatrist David Henderson published his *Psychopathic States* (Henderson, 1939). Henderson drew attention to the neglected focus on the psychopathic personality's ability to appear quite normal psychologically as they go about their egocentric ways. This ability to avoid detection, through charm and calculated, carefully crafted behavior, has come to be one of the most recognized features of the modern construct of "psychopathy." As we will see in the following chapter, it is this ability to go undetected that has allowed psychopathic personalities like Corporate Psychopaths to flourish in large business organizations. In 1941, Hervey Cleckley, staff psychiatrist at a Georgia Veterans Administration hospital, published *The Mask of Sanity: An Attempt to Reinterpret Some Issues About the So-Called Psychopathic Personality*. The *Mask of Sanity*, and the account of the psychopathic personality Cleckley developed therein, became the greatest influence on the study of psychopathy as it picked up academic and clinical steam during the later decades of the 20th century.

Cleckley's theory of psychopathy emerged from his study of the case histories of 15 individuals (13 men and two women) whom he argued represented the prototypical psychopathic personality, along with several cases of "incomplete manifestations or suggestions of the disorder" (Cleckley, 1941, p. xiii). In the first edition of *The Mask of Sanity*, Cleckley identified 21 core traits which, when taken collectively, distinguish the psychopathic personality. In later additions, the list was shortened to 16 core personality traits, which have come to be known as the "Cleckley criteria." These are (a) superficial charm and good "intelligence"; (b) absence of delusions and other signs of irrational thinking; (c) absence of nervousness and psychoneurotic manifestations; (d) unreliability; (e) untruthfulness and insincerity; (f) lack of remorse or shame; (g) inadequately motivated antisocial behavior; (h) poor judgment and failure to learn by experience; (i) pathological egocentricity and incapacity for love; (j) general poverty in major affective reactions; (k) specific loss of insight; (l) unresponsiveness in general interpersonal relations; (m) fantastic and uninviting behavior with drink and sometimes without; (n) suicide rarely carried out; (o) sex life impersonal, trivial, and poorly integrated; and (p) failure to follow any life plan (Cleckley, 1941, pp. 338–339). Cleckley's purpose was to reign in the loose usage of the label "psychopathy" that had become the norm by specifying in detail the distinctive psychological components of the particular manifestation of antisocial behavior that would come to be understood as "psychopathy" proper. Most striking, Cleckley described, is the "psychopath's" ability to appear charming, poised, and intellectual to others while harboring an "inner self" entirely consumed by affective disorders and a lack of effective impulse controls that prevent them from entering into authentic interpersonal relationships. He wrote, ". . . the central personality 'lesions' of the psychopath are not covered over by peripheral or surface functioning suggestive of some eccentricity or peculiarity of personality but by a perfect mask of genuine sanity, a flawless surface indicative in every respect of robust mental health" (Cleckley, 1941, p. 253), all the while "masking" a complete absence of the basic affective capacities central to the conduct of a moral life, This inner moral void eventually shows itself in outbursts of egregious antisocial behavior. To this day, field and laboratory research in the area of psychopathy study are grounded in the "Cleckley criteria."

Robert Hare, emeritus professor of psychology at the University of British Columbia, is credited with refining Cleckley's insights, and criteria, into a working clinical definition of psychopathy starting with the publication of his *Psychopathy: Theory and Research* in 1970, which drew together previous work in the field of psychopathy study and sought to clarify the construct of "psychopathy." He published his diagnostic tool, the Psychopathy Checklist (PCL) in 1980, which has since gone through a number of revisions (the current version is referred to as the PCL-R). Hare's interest in the study of psychopathy was triggered during an eight-month stint as a prison psychologist in Vancouver, British Columbia in 1960. This interest turned into a career-long research specialty beginning in 1963 when, as a member of the psychology department at the University of British Columbia, he discovered that the psychopathic personalities he studied did not evince the same stress-induced, physiological reactions to anticipated electric shocks as non-psychopathic criminals and community control groups.

Hare originally expanded the "Cleckley criteria" into a set of 22 distinct criteria in his PCL, but later trimmed the set down to 20 in the PCL-R. Though he is most well-known for developing a diagnostic tool for identifying psychopathy in forensic and clinical settings, Hare is also known for setting the stage for, some would say, the most pressing debate within the contemporary psychology of psychopathy; namely, the debate as to which aspect of psychopathy to emphasize: the personality or the behavior. As Harris, Skilling, and Rice describe it,

> . . . Hare and his colleagues identified two related aspects of psychopathy: an affective/interpersonal dimension characterized by shallowness, callousness, remorselessness, and dishonesty; and a behavioral, lifestyle component characterized by juvenile delinquency, criminal versatility, irresponsibility, sensation seeking, and impulsivity . . . The most hotly debated issues concerned whether diagnosis should be based on personality or behavior, whether the personality factor predicted violent recidivism better than the behavioral factor, whether measurement of the first factor yielded better psychometric properties than the second, and whether some particular psychophysiological measure is related more to one factor than the other. (2001, p. 204).

Later in this chapter, we will examine the historical relationship between the development of the *Diagnostic and Statistical Manual of Mental Disorders* (*DSM*), the taxonomic and diagnostic tool published by the American Psychiatric Association, and ongoing calls for psychopathy to be included in the *DSM* as a distinct mental disorder. Through multiple revisions of the *DSM*, Hare and others advocating his two-factor approach to describing the phenomenon of psychopathy have continued lobbying for greater emphasis to be placed on the affective/interpersonal factor over the behavioral factor. Over the years, this position has remained at odds with the series of *DSM* authors who have held solid to the position that the behavioral factor be given greater weight. This dispute has remained the major reason that "psychopathy" has yet to show up in the *DSM* as a distinct personality disorder diagnosis.

Hare was also a pathbreaker in bringing the psychology of psychopathy to the attention of the general public with two "popular science" books, one published in 1993 and the other in 2006. In *Without Conscience: The Disturbing World of the Psychopaths Among Us* (1993 and reissue), Hare brought to the public's attention the fact that most "psychopaths," though social predators, do not wind up as criminal murderers. It provided a summary of what was known about "psychopaths" at the time through the use of anecdotes, some of them graphic, which fit in well with the popular sensationalism already attending psychopathy occasioned by the release of *The Silence of the Lambs* two years earlier. In *Snakes in Suits: When Psychopaths Go to Work* (2006), co-authored with organizational psychologist and human resources consultant Paul Babiak, Hare put discussion of Corporate Psychopaths squarely in the public eye. Babiak and Hare's account of "successful psychopaths" and the damage they can do to business organizations sounded the alarm for the "seek and destroy" element of the Corporate Psychopath Hypothesis.

THE CONTEMPORARY TAKE ON PSYCHOPATHY

Due to media focus on cases of violent psychopathic personalities such as serial killers and sexual predators, and the manner in which popular culture tends to portray them (e.g., Hannibal Lecter from *The Silence of the Lambs*), the general public tends to regard such presentations as the archetypal psychopathic personality. As Clarke notes, however, "While violent criminal psychopaths unquestionably exist, they are a minority of the psychopath population" (Clarke, 2005, p. 29). In support of the Corporate Psychopath Hypothesis, Clarke provides this warning:

> The images and stereotypes of psychopaths that we are given by the media is the contemporary equivalent of the belief in werewolves. We might think that the serial killer or rapist is terrifying and unpredictable, but it is the psychopath in our workplace who threatens our personal and psychological safety, who is far more common than we are led to believe. (Clarke, 2005, pp. 29–30).

There is also a tendency in the popular treatment of psychopathy to confuse it with sociopathy. In *Snakes and Suits*, Babiak and Hare provide the following explanation of the differences between psychopathy and sociopathy:

> *Psychopathy* is a personality disorder described by the personality traits and behaviors that form the basis of this book. Psychopaths are without conscience and incapable of empathy, guilt, or loyalty to anyone but themselves.
>
> *Sociopathy* . . . refers to patterns of attitudes and behaviors that are considered antisocial and criminal by society at large, but are seen as normal or necessary by the subculture or social environment in which they developed. Sociopaths may have a well-developed conscience and a normal capacity for empathy, guilt, and loyalty, but their sense of right and wrong is based on the norms and expectations of their subculture or group. (Babiak & Hare, 2006, p. 19)

As noted above, contemporary work in the psychology of psychopathy stems from Hare's work begun in the 1970s, which itself is, in a substantial sense, a refined extension of Cleckley's work. Recall the 16 traits Cleckley cites as the core of the psychopathic personality:

1. superficial charm and good "intelligence"
2. absence of delusions and other signs of irrational thinking

3. absence of nervousness and psychoneurotic manifestations
4. unreliability
5. untruthfulness and insincerity
6. lack of remorse or shame
7. inadequately motivated antisocial behavior
8. poor judgment and failure to learn by experience
9. pathological egocentricity and incapacity for love
10. general poverty in major affective reactions
11. specific loss of insight
12. unresponsiveness in general interpersonal relations
13. fantastic and uninviting behavior with drink and sometimes without
14. suicide rarely carried out
15. sex life impersonal, trivial, and poorly integrated
16. failure to follow any life plan

Cleckley's experience with psychopathic psychiatric patients revealed a remarkable ability on the part of psychopathic personalities to appear normal, at least for an extended time, hence, the "mask of sanity." This ability to remain hidden from view is regarded as a defining feature in particular of Corporate Psychopaths. It also led him to the conclusion that psychopathy was not treatable, though he was hopeful that future advances in psychiatric treatments might remedy this situation.

Hare, who frequently communicated with Cleckley, originally expanded the "Cleckley criteria" to a total of 22 distinct criteria for psychopathy, but later trimmed the total down to 20 traits to be measured by the PCL-R.

1. glib and superficial charm
2. grandiose (exaggeratedly high) estimation of self
3. need for stimulation
4. pathological lying
5. cunning and manipulativeness
6. lack of remorse or guilt
7. shallow affect (superficial emotional responsiveness)
8. callousness and lack of empathy
9. parasitic lifestyle
10. poor behavioral controls
11. sexual promiscuity
12. early behavior problems
13. lack of realistic long-term goals
14. impulsivity
15. irresponsibility

16. failure to accept responsibility for own actions
17. many short-term marital relationships
18. juvenile delinquency
19. revocation of conditional release
20. criminal versatility

Like Cleckley, Hare too drew attention to the psychopathic personality's remarkable ability to hide in plain sight, hence "snakes in suits."

The 20-item list of traits to be assessed for in PCL-R psychopathy screening was originally divided by Hare into two "factor groups." Factor one traits, such as superficial charm, manipulativeness, and lack of empathy, are grouped as affective/interpersonal deficits. Factor two traits, such as criminal versatility, impulsiveness, and irresponsibility, are grouped as symptoms relating to impulsivity-antisocial behavior. This two-factor model came under criticism in the late 1990s and early 2000s based on studies done of male prisoners in a mental health unit, prisoners with substance abuse disorders, forensic psychiatric samples, and female offenders (Vitacco et al., 2005, p. 467). These studies indicated that the two-factor model of psychopathy failed the confirmatory factor analysis test in the populations studied (i.e., the unobserved, latent factors of the model failed to explain the correlations among indicators and observed behavior). In its place, a four-factor model has been developed sorting the PCL-R traits into the categories of *Interpersonal* (e.g., superficial charm, grandiosity, and deceitfulness), *Affective* (e.g., lack of remorse and empathy), *Lifestyle* (e.g., impulsivity and irresponsibility), and *Antisocial* (e.g., absence of behavioral controls) (Mathieu et al., 2013, p. 289). Debate is ongoing regarding which multiple factor model best represents the construct of "psychopathy" in laboratory and field research, mainly around the question of including or not including the antisocial factor in the model. This question is important for the Corporate Psychopath Hypothesis in that Corporate Psychopaths typically do not display the types of behavior listed as "antisocial"; that is one of the reasons they are adept at remaining undetected.

For Hare, it is the "affective/interpersonal" factor that marks off psychopathy as a distinct mental disorder. As will be described in greater detail below, it is this focus on the nonbehavioral aspects of psychopathy that is at the center of the debate between the advocates for listing psychopathy as a distinct, clinically diagnostic disorder and the authors of the *DSM*. Advocates for treating psychopathy as a mental disorder unto itself do not dismiss the role of antisocial behavior in both the lives of psychopathic personalities and the diagnosis of psychopathy, but such antisocial behavior can coexist with other mental disorders such as narcissistic personality disorder, anxiety disorder, and sadistic personality disorder. A complete or strong focus on antisocial behavior, at the expense of the affective/interpersonal factor, as the determinative diagnostic factor fails to identify what it is about psychopathic personalities that cause them to, at times, engage in antisocial behavior. If the Corporate Psychopath Hypothesis is correct, then such a diagnostic focus will "miss" an entire subgroup of psychopathic personalities.

Others contributing to the literature on the Corporate Psychopath Hypothesis have offered their own list of core psychopathic personality traits. Clarke, for example, provides a rather lengthy list of the personality traits and antisocial behaviors that go into diagnoses of psychopathy (Clarke, 2005, p. 23).

Table 1.1.

Lack of remorse or guilt	criminal behavior	impersonal sex life
Impulsive behavior	lack of responsibility	prolific lying/deception
Manipulation of others	lack of conscience	superficial charm
Unreliability	insincerity	antisocial behavior
Poor judgment	incapacity for love	lack of emotion
Absence of life goals	checkered employment history	
Constant need for stimulation	failure to learn by experience	

The construct of "psychopathy" has always been understood to be a *dimensional* construct, not a *categorical* one. It is based on a cluster of personality traits, with variations in the particular array of traits that an individual psychopathic personality may exhibit and in the intensity of each of the traits present. To be judged "psychopathic" based on a PCL-R score, an individual need not display each of the 20 personality and behavioral traits assessed for, and need not be rated to have each trait that is present in their psychopathic profile to the highest degree (the PCL-R uses a 0–2 rating scale where a rating of "0" indicates a judgment that the trait is not present, a rating of "1" indicates a judgment that the trait is partially present, and a rating of "2" indicates that the trait is clearly present). A diagnosis of "psychopathy" is not based on a singular set of necessary and sufficient conditions. The dimensionality of the construct is reflected not only in the fact that psychopathic personalities can display different specific trait profiles, but also in the fact that, though a score of 30 or higher on the PCL-R is treated as the threshold for a diagnosis of psychopathy, individuals approaching that threshold but not reaching it may be psychopathic enough to elicit concern. Though, in this text, we are reserving use of the label "psychopathic personality" for individuals reaching the PCL-R threshold, it must be acknowledged that because "psychopathy" is understood in terms of a multi-factor continuum there is some inherent "looseness" to the construct in that it can be applied appropriately to noticeably different individual personalities. Though both receive official designations as "psychopathic," an individual scoring a perfect 40 on the PCL-R will be strikingly different from an individual scoring 30 or in the high 20s. The subjectivity introduced by the need for trained, experienced psychologists or psychiatrists to administer and interpret the results of the PCL-R adds to the dimensionality of the construct in that, even if reliable, there will be some differences between raters' judgments.

On the subject of psychopathic personalities in the workplace, Clarke divides them into four groups:

> *The Organizational Psychopath*—they manipulate their way into top management positions for the rewards and power that such positions confer and to take pleasure in the suffering and misery they cause to others along the way
>
> *The Corporate Criminal Psychopath*—they commit criminal acts through the positions they hold within their profession (e.g., bank employers, stockbrokers, or lawyers) in order to enhance their own financial status at the expense of their clients or the firm they work for
>
> *The Violent Criminal Psychopath*—they are the media portrayed archetypal "psychopath," holding down a job and going undetected until apprehended for some violent act
>
> *The Occupational Psychopath*—they use their occupation to satisfy their desire to bully or intimidate others while avoiding punishment for doing so (e.g., an army officer who bullies subordinates but is able to "write it off" as part of their occupational duty). (Clarke, 2005, pp. 55–74)

It is the organizational psychopaths and corporate criminal psychopaths who are the subject of the Corporate Psychopath Hypothesis, though that is not to say that one might not encounter the Corporate Psychopath in the form of the occupational psychopath.

It must be recognized that there is not unanimity in the community of psychology researchers and clinicians regarding the modern construct of "psychopathy." For some, Hare's understanding of the psychopathic personality has internal problems. For example, that view of psychopathic personalities emphasizes the belief that such personalities are incapable of experiencing a range of emotions and lack remorse, guilt, and regret, and that they are also entirely lacking in the capacity for empathy. Some research is emerging, however, leading psychologists to reexamine this part of the psychopathic personality profile. In a study of 62 male adults recruited through flyers soliciting risk-taking (e.g., crime, substance use, gambling, impulsive behavior, bullying), half of whom had been incarcerated previous to participation in the study, Baskin-Sommers, Stuppy-Sullivan, and Buckholtz placed the participants in a gambling situation where they were asked to pick one of two wheels, each with two possible outcomes (e.g., –75 and +75) and, based on the amount of each wheel covered by the outcome, each with varying probabilities of any particular outcome (Baskin-Sommers et al., 2013). Participants selected a wheel, and a ball dropped onto the wheel and moved around roulette-style before dropping into an outcome section. Immediately after each spin, participants were asked to rate their regret on their choice of wheels along a continuum from "very disappointed" to "very pleased." The Self-Report Psychopathy–III scale was used to rate the psychopathic profiles of the participants. The results indicated that participants scoring higher on the SRP-III did show signs of experiencing regret over their decisions, but only a particular type of regret. In an interview with the *Harvard Gazette*, Buckholtz put it this way:

> There are two components to regret, there is retrospective regret, which is how we usually think about regret—the emotional experience after you learn you could have received a better outcome if you had made a different choice. But we also use signals from our environment to make predictions about which actions will or won't result in regret. What differentiated psychopaths from other people was their inability to use those prospective regret signals, to use information about the choices they were given to anticipate how much regret they were going to experience, and adjust their decision-making accordingly.
>
> It's almost like a blindness to future regret, when something happens, they feel regret, but what they can't do is look forward and use information that would tell them they're going to feel regret to guide their decision-making. (Reuell, 2017)

There are critics of the construct of psychopathy, not just of any particular conception of what is involved in a diagnosis of "psychopathy," but of the entire construct itself. Some, such as Lewis, argue that diagnoses of psychopathy are too subjective since they are dependent on raters or self-reporting or third-party reports, and too shallow, failing to take advantage of comprehensive psychiatric evaluations that if engaged in, would reveal the "real" disorders in place that give rise to the personality traits constitutive of psychopathy.

> The concept and subsequent reification of the diagnosis "psychopathy" has, to this author's mind, hampered the understanding of criminality and violence... According to Hare, in many cases one need not even meet the patient. Just rummage through his records to determine what items seemed to fit. Nonsense. To this writer's mind, psychopathy and its synonyms (e.g., sociopathy and antisocial personality) are lazy diagnoses. Over the years the authors' team has seen scores of offenders who, prior to evaluation by the authors, were dismissed

> as psychopaths or the like. Detailed, comprehensive psychiatric, neurological, and neuropsychological evaluations have uncovered a multitude of signs, symptoms, and behaviors indicative of such disorders as bipolar mood disorder, schizophrenia spectrum disorders, complex partial seizures, dissociative identity disorder, parasomnia, and, of course, brain damage/dysfunction. (Lewis, 2017, p. 2425)

In reference to research that indicates a lack of reliability for the PCL-R as a screening instrument, Martens draws attention to the misuse that can result from a reliance on the PCL-R as an indicator of the presence of psychopathy, especially given the serious, negative outcomes for individuals labelled "psychopathic" in legal proceedings:

> Situations in which the prediction of "future dangerousness" is at issue appear to be logical areas in which the assessment of psychopathic traits would be relevant to decision making. One recent application of psychopathy has been its inclusion in death penalty cases, where Psychopathy Checklist-Revised (PCL-R) scores have been introduced to support the position that a defendant will represent a "continuing threat" to society—even if serving a life sentence in prison. Despite such claims, a review of the relevant research indicates that the empirical basis for these conclusions is minimal at present. The PCL-R can be misused and misrepresented in legal settings. Moreover, because of the considerable implications of the "psychopathy" diagnosis in forensic contexts, misuse of this instrument could be especially damaging to the integrity of the adjudicative process. (Martens, 2008, p. 454)

The matter of the reliability and validity of psychopathy screening instruments will be taken up in more detail in chapter four, when we turn to a consideration of the ethical issues associated with employment screening for psychopathy. Hare and other defenders of the PCL-R and its derivative versions such as the PCL:SV have claimed both reliability and validity for those instruments, as have designers of other screening tools. For critics, the absence of a reliable and valid measurement tool implies that psychopathy may not indeed be a useful psychological construct inasmuch as there is no scientifically appropriate way to identify its existence. All that can be concluded at this point is that it remains an open question.

Despite these criticisms, "psychopathy" remains a much discussed psychological construct. One can find varying definitions of "psychopathy" in the literature, typically shortened versions of the items on Hare's Checklist. Recognizing that "psychopathy" is a dimensional construct, there is no "typical" psychopathic personality. Yet, there are core traits that are distinctive of psychopathic personalities (those scoring 30 or higher on the PCL-R, for example): glib and superficial charm, egocentricity, lack of affective states such as remorse and guilt, and an apparent inability to either experience empathy for others or be concerned about their inability to do so. A propensity for antisocial behavior is part of the core of psychopathy, with the caveat that not all psychopathic personalities will engage in repetitive acts of egregious antisocial behavior such as violence or criminal activity. Corporate Psychopaths in particular are less prone to engaging in such stark forms of antisocial behavior, one reason why they exist undetected in organizations for lengthy periods of time. The dimensionality of the psychopathy construct is something that leaves room for doubt regarding psychopathy's status as a mental illness or disorder. If a psychopathic personality shares types of personality traits with non-psychopathic personalities, if it is just that they have them to a heightened degree or level of intensity, then we are talking about degrees of difference, not categorical differences. In what way, one could ask, would a psychopathic personality be *ill* or *disordered*, rather than just *different*? One of the criticisms of the Hare model of psychopathy is that it focuses exclusively on the maladaptive aspects of the cluster of personality traits constitutive of psychopathy while overlooking the fact that many individuals with those traits are able to adapt to the presence of some or many of those traits and manage them in positive ways so that they do not issue in disordered behavior (they are often referred to as "functioning psychopaths," a subject that will be discussed in greater detail in chapter four). In its infancy as a psychological construct, Cleckley recognized this fact and further grouped his 16 criteria for diagnosing psychopathy into three categories based on the extent to which the personality traits present issued in positive social functioning, or behavior characterized by disinhibited and antisocial tendencies, or behavior that reflected disturbed interpersonal functioning. If similar clusters of psychopathic personality traits can be found in both normally functioning individuals and in highly aberrant individuals, then why is psychopathy itself a "disorder?"

This way of thinking about the matter, however, ignores the fact that we do judge differences of degree in other scenarios to be grounds for calling the extraordinary case an illness or disorder. Alcoholism, for example. It is the case that people have a desire to drink alcohol to varying degrees, with some, diagnosed alcoholics, having an irresistible desire to do so. Yet, the American Medical Association, the American College of Physicians, the U.S. National Institutes for Health, and the World Health Organization all recognize alcoholism as a disease. Body temperature is another example. There is a normal range for human bodily temperature and an abnormal range, the latter treated as an illness even though, no pun intended, we are talking about a difference in degree. So, the fact that psychopathy is treated as a dimensional construct, not a categorical one, doesn't rule out the possibility of treating psychopathy as an illness or disorder.

The other major type of argument against the view that psychopathy should be regarded as a mental illness or disorder relies on the consideration that the presence of psychopathic personalities in human populations has been historically stable. Recalling the brief history of psychopathy presented above, observers as far back as ancient Greece have identified individuals who, if they were alive today, would likely qualify as psychopathic. Given this fact, the argument goes, psychopathy must not be as serious a mental disorder or illness as contemporary commentators make it out to be. Recently, Jurjako has claimed that from an evolutionary biology perspective, psychopathy should not be thought of as a maladaptive mental disorder. Instead, "psychopathic individuals might be psychologically and biologically equipped for instantiating a reproductive strategy that is maintained by a frequency-dependent selection and is prosperous in harsh environments where it pays off to exhibit antisocial personality traits" (Jurjako, 2019, p. 2). He employs Wakefield's Harmful Dysfunction view of mental disorders developed in the early 1990's, which sets the following conditions for categorization as a mental disorder:

> A condition is a disorder if and only if (a) the condition causes some harm or deprivation of benefit to the person as judged by the standards of the person's culture (the value criterion), and (b) the condition results from the inability of some internal mechanism to perform its natural function, wherein natural function is an effect that is part of the evolutionary explanation of the existence and structure of the mechanism (the explanatory criterion). (Wakefield, 1992, p. 384)

Psychopathy easily satisfies the "harmful condition" criterion, as Jurjako acknowledges. Though psychopathic personalities may not experience "subjective distress" due to their psychopathy, they, at least in the vast majority of cases, are deprived of access to socially desirable goods such as freedom, meaningful relationships, romance, community membership, and social recognition. The case for psychopathy satisfying the "dysfunction" criterion is not so easily made, Jurjako argues. Drawing upon a vein of psychopathy research that explains the historically stable presence of psychopathy in human populations as an adaptation to certain "ecological and social niches" (see, for example, Jonason et al., and Schmitt 2009; Jonason et al., 2010; Krupp et al., 2013; Lykken, 1995; and Meloy et al., 2018), Jurjako argues that as long as the percentage of psychopathic individuals in a population remains fairly low (so as to not raise any general alarm in the population) and that population is generally "social" in its interactions (e.g., regularly cooperates with one another in honest and trusting ways), the small number of psychopathic personalities can gain some advantage by being "antisocial." For example, "psychopaths' promiscuous and early onset of sexual behavior and many short-term marital relationships could increase the probability of reproductive and mating success; glibness/superficial charm would enable psychopaths to navigate social structures undetected, allow them to deceive others, present themselves as socially attractive and attract or poach potential mates" (Jurjako, 2019, p. 14). Some recent research provides support for the claim that psychopathy is a "niche adaptation" because it yields sustainable reproductive success (Neumann et al., 2012; Međedović et al., 2017). Seen as a "positive adaptation," it is difficult, Jurjako concludes, to regard it as an illness or disorder.

Of course, there are equally vocal defenders of the view that psychopathy is a mental disorder. Blair very boldly proclaims psychopathy to be a "cognitive and neural dysfunction" and a "developmental disorder" (Blair, 2013). As Brazil and Cima describe in their review of contemporary approaches to psychopathy, there are other approaches to the study of psychopathy that focus on "cognitive and/or neurobiological" models of psychopathy, rather than traditional, personality-based models (Brazil & Cima, 2016). One cognitive-based model that has received considerable attention since the mid-1990's is the "low-fear" account of psychopathy popularized by Lykken in the 1990s (Lykken, 1995), and since bolstered by empirical research indicating that psychopathic personalities show reduced fear responsivity and fear-conditioning resulting in maladaptive social behavior (Birbaumer et al., 2005; Flor et al., 2002). A second cognitive model, the "response modulation hypothesis," is intended to capture research indicating that psychopathic personalities have broader information processing deficiencies than just those related to fear processing. The response modulation hypothesis "attributes the disinhibition seen in psychopathy to a failure to shift attention automatically from the implementation of ongoing goal-directed behavior to its evaluation" (Hamilton & Newman, 2018 81). This failure to shift to a consideration of secondary, evaluative information results in a much lower ability to act in cognitively inhibited ways. Blair suggests that an underlying neurobiological component of this attention failure in psychopathic personalities may be found in increased priming of "task-relevant representations" by the lateral frontal, dorsomedial, and parietal cortices, which decreases the strength of secondary emotional stimuli leading to decreased amygdala responses to these stimuli (Blair, 2013, p. 183). A third model, the "integrated emotion systems" model, is a neurobiology-based model. As Brazil and Cima sum it up, "The premise [of the IES model] is that psychopathic individuals are less capable of linking negative outcomes (e.g., loss of money) and the corresponding negative affective states (e.g., feeling sad about losing money) to the event that led to the negative outcome" (Brazil & Cima, 2016, p. 215). This lack of "emotional integration" is believed to be due to deficient functioning of the amygdala and other prefrontal brain regions. For all three models, psychopathy is regarded as a "malfunctioning" of cognition, perhaps grounded in neurobiological dysfunction (more will be said about research on the neurobiological foundations of psychopathy in chapter three). In this way, they are models intended to describe the core psychological mechanism at the heart of psychopathy and to present that mechanism as a disordered departure from normal cognitive and/or neurobiological functioning.

Whether it is correct to treat psychopathy as a mental disorder or impairment remains a scientifically unsettled question. As Reimer has argued, this ongoing dispute may be a function of the "value-laden" language that gets employed in the arguments themselves (Reimer, 2008). For example, researchers like Blair talk about "brain *dysfunction*," not "brain *differences*," and the PCL-R uses language like "*pathological* lying" and "*parasitic* life-style," both phrases heavily laden in normative terms. The importance of the question, however, is not in dispute. As noted above, whether psychopathy is to be regarded as a mental disorder influences legal accountability and sentencing processes. It also has an impact on clinical treatment protocols. As we will see in chapter three, a positive stance on the question brings into play the possibility that psychopathic personalities may qualify as "disabled" individuals under the Americans with Disabilities Act. So, it is not a trivial or esoteric question. It has implications that extend beyond the professions of psychology and psychiatry. For the sake of the argument advanced in chapter three, that it is reasonable to believe that psychopathic personalities would be covered under the ADA, it is necessary to be able to classify psychopathy as at least an *impairment*, though it isn't necessary that psychopathy be grounded in some cognitive or neurological *dysfunction or disorder*, though the evidence marshalled in support of such a claim cannot be ignored as it does provide further credence to the legal argument developed in chapter three. The language of the ADA and various ADA-related EEOC guidelines provide for a way to interpret "impairment" that doesn't require independent proof of the presence of a "disorder." As for the ethical arguments against employment screening for psychopathy, to be developed in chapter four, it is not at all necessary that psychopathy be grounded in a cognitive or neurological dysfunction, or be an impairment of some kind. In the context of the arguments advanced there, it is perfectly sufficient if psychopathy is treated simply as a *difference*, not a disorder. It is important in many other respects that the question about the "disordered" status of psychopathy be settled, but for the purposes of this text, we can, to a degree, remain agnostic about that.

PSYCHOPATHY SCREENING INSTRUMENTS

Though for some the construct of "psychopathy" still remains ill-defined, confusing, "unscientific," and susceptible to misuse, there is no shortage of psychopathy screening instruments out there. These screening instruments fall into two categories: expert rater devices, like Hare's PCL-R, and self-report inventories like Levenson's Self-Report Psychopathy Scale. Hare's PCL-R is regarded by most clinicians and researchers as the "gold standard" for identifying psychopathic personalities. He has, over the years, developed "smaller" versions of the PCL-R, such as the PCL:SV and the B-Scan. The PCL-R is designed for use in clinical, legal, or research settings. Though originally intended to be an assessment of the extent, if any, of an individual's psychopathic personality, it has also come to be used as an indicator of the potential risk a subject or criminal poses. There are two parts to the PCL-R: a semi-structured interview and a review of the subject's history, including any available file records. The interview portion involves questions about the subject's background, including items like past personal relationships, educational and employment history, and criminal activity. Information gleaned from the interview is compared with data from file records for corroboration since psychopathic personalities are at ease with lying. The rater then assigns a 0–2 score for each of the 20 traits assessed. A "perfect" would be 40. The threshold for designations as "psychopathic" is 30. Hare has developed derivative screening instruments like the PCL:SV (*Psychopathy Checklist Screening Version*) and the B-Scan (*Business-Scan*). The PCL:SV employs a 12-item checklist, conceptually and empirically related to the PCL-R, and is intended for use in civil psychiatric and community populations. Its application is the same as that for the PCL-R with the advantage of requiring less time and resources to complete. Designed for use in corporate and organizational settings, the B-Scan, the most recent derivative of the PCL-R, relies on the same 20-item list as the PCL-R, but involves a 360-degree evaluative element drawn from reports from supervisors, peers, and subordinates. This addition is intended to overcome two challenges: it is quite difficult to get organizations to participate in studies intended to identify psychopathic personalities in their midst, and there is facility at lying that psychopathic personalities display in face-to-face interviews.

Boddy has developed his own screening instrument, derived from Hare's PCL-R, for use specifically in identifying Corporate Psychopaths. The Psychopathy Measure–Management Research Version (PM-MRV), measures for the eight items Hare has suggested are definitive of Corporate Psychopaths: (1) are glib and superficially charming, (2) have a grandiose sense of self-worth, (3) are accomplished liars, (4) are manipulative and conning, (5) display a lack of remorse about how their actions harm other employees, (6) are emotionally shallow, calculating, and cold, (7) display a lack of empathy; show no capacity to experience the feelings of others, and (8) refuse to take responsibility for their own actions (Boddy, 2011b, p. 14). The PM-MRV uses eight items from the PCL-R associated with the *Affective* and *Interpersonal* dimensions of psychopathy and uses the same 0–2 scoring system. It does not involve an interview with subjects; instead it relies on the reports of co-workers in the form of responses to questions directed at their experiences of behavior associated with psychopathic personalities. Corporate Psychopaths are designated by this measure to be individuals who score 13 or higher out of a possible score of 16.

Developed in 1995 for use in research settings, the Levenson Self-Report Psychopathy Scale (LSRP) measures psychopathy on two scales: primary psychopathy (psychopathic emotional affect) and secondary psychopathy (psychopathic lifestyle). It uses a self-completion survey consisting of twenty six statements, such as "For me what's right is what I can get away with," "Looking out for myself is my top priority," "I find myself in the same kinds of trouble time and time again," and "I am often bored," that could possibly apply to the taker of the survey. Respondents rate each statement on the extent to which they agree with it on a scale of (1) strongly disagree, (2) disagree, (3) neither agree nor disagree, (4) agree, or (5) strongly agree. There is an online version of the LSRP that, its creators tout, only takes around five minutes to complete. The LSRP is purposely intended only for research purposes. It is not intended to be used for diagnostic purposes. As such, there is no "score threshold" to be met to qualify as a psychopathic personality per se. Instead, it generates means for both primary and secondary psychopathy to which individual respondents can be compared. Another popular self-reporting instrument is the Psychopathic Personality Inventory (PPI-Revised), developed by Lillienfeld and Andrews to be used in noncriminal populations. Like the LSRP, the PPI-Revised is a self-reporting instrument in which respondents use a 4-point Likert scale ("False," "Mostly False," "Mostly True," or "True") to respond to a 154-item self-referential questionnaire.

Concerns over the validation of the PCL-R, and hence any other screening instruments directly derived from it, were mentioned above. These same concerns, and others, are present when assessing self-reporting measurement instruments like the LSRP and the PPI-Revised. These concerns are critical to any discussion about the legitimacy of the psychopathy construct. Until, or unless, they can be addressed, doubts will remain about the scientific validity and usefulness of the use of the construct. For the purposes of this text, the reliability question need not be settled. It is not the author's intent to critically assess the psychopathy construct *itself*. Rather, it is our aim to grant, for the most part, the psychological underpinnings of the construct so as to address a particular set of ethical issues occasioned by the Corporate Psychopath Hypothesis, which itself is grounded in the psychology of psychopathy.

PSYCHOPATHY AND THE DSM

The *Diagnostic and Statistical Manual of Mental Disorders* (*DSM*), published by the American Psychiatric Association (APA), is the most commonly used clinical manual for diagnosing mental disorders in the U.S. Internationally, the *International Classification of Diseases and Related Health Problems* (*ICD*), published by the World Health Organization, is more widely used primarily because of its broader scope (it covers overall health, not just mental health) and the role it plays in global policy-making. There have been seven editions of the *DSM*, two of which are revised versions of previously published editions: *DSM-I* (1952), *DSM-II* (1968), *DSM-III* (1980), *DSM-III-R* (1987), *DSM-IV* (1994), *DSM-IV-TR* (2000), and *DSM-V* (2013). The *DSM* defines and classifies mental disorders using a standard language and classificatory system. It is used by clinicians and researchers to diagnose patients and in the conduct of forensic studies. Health care regulatory agencies rely upon the *DSM* classificatory schema to set the prescription protocols for drugs intended to treat clinically diagnosable mental disorders, and pharmaceutical companies tailor their research and development efforts to conform to the *DSM* list of recognized mental disorders. As we will see in chapter three, courts have deferred to appeals to the *DSM* in sentencing proceedings. Though over the years more consistency and overlap between the *DSM* and the *ICD* has emerged, some noticeable content differences between the two remain. For the purposes of this work, we will exclusively reference the *DSM*.

As Crego and Widiger note, "the construct of psychopathy has had a troubled, and at times controversial, relationship" with the *DSM* (Crego & Widiger, 2015, p. 665). At the heart of this "troubled and controversial" relationship is an ongoing dispute about the relative significance to attach to either behavioral patterns or affective, trait-based criteria for diagnosis of antisocial personality disorder (ASPD), and whether psychopathy is itself a single disorder within a unitary etiology or, rather, a constellation of traits each with its own etiology. Through five editions of the *DSM*, the ASPD construct has retained a behavioral bent, though an attempt at a "hybrid" approach can be seen in the current edition of the *DSM*, the *DSM-V* (2013), and has consistently treated psychopathy as a particular instantiation of ASPD, a "specifier" of ASPD, but not a clinically described disorder in itself.

In its first edition, published in 1952, the *DSM* included what it labelled "sociopathic personality disturbance," which it designated as inclusive of cases previously labelled as "constitutional psychopathic state" and "psychopathic personality" (Cleckley's language). The *DSM-II* (1968) expanded the description of "antisocial personality" to include most of the personality traits Cleckley had associated with "psychopathic personality" over twenty years earlier. However, beginning with the *DSM-III* (1980), the clinical model moved away from one wherein clinicians made diagnoses of ASPD by matching what they knew about a client to a narrative-based, prototypical case to one wherein clinicians could reference a set of "objective," behavior-centered criteria, which included conduct disorder, relationship infidelity or instability, financial irresponsibility, and recklessness (APA, 1980). In effect, it was a shift away from the trait-focused approach pioneered by Cleckley and the continuation of that approach being further developed at the time by Hare. Though authors of later editions of the *DSM* tried to "reconcile" an objective, behavior-focused diagnostic approach to ASPD with the less overt, trait-inference approach developed by Hare and preferred by many clinicians, the APA construct of ASPD maintained its separation from PCL-R-defined psychopathy. In principle, this effort was intended to reduce the unreliability of mental disorder diagnoses based solely on the subjective judgments of individual clinicians by replacing that practice with one grounded in a set of universal diagnostic guidelines.

It was within this setting that ASPD emerged as what Crego and Widiger call the "poster child" for the success of the new objective approach to mental disorder diagnosis (Crego & Widiger, 2015, p. 666). A nine-item criteria list for ASPD diagnosis was set: (1) conduct disorder, which was required, (2) poor work history, (3) irresponsible parent, (4) unlawful behavior, (5) relationship infidelity or instability, (6) aggressiveness, (7) financial irresponsibility, (8) no regard for the truth, and (9) recklessness (APA, 1980). Regarding diagnoses of psychopathy as a particular specifier of ASPD, one broad criticism that has remained is that the *DSM* approach requires that an explicit set of behaviors be present in order to infer the presence of personality traits. Hare's work developing the PCL-R, which happened concurrently with the crafting of the *DSM-III*, relied on directly identifying those traits definitive of psychopathy, whether or not individuals being diagnosed had engaged in the range of behaviors, including the required "conduct disorder." Given an emphasis on criminal behavior in particular, Hare remarked at the time that "*DSM-III* has difficulty in identifying individuals who fit the classic picture of psychopathy but who manage to avoid early or formal contact with the criminal justice system" (Hare, 1986, p. 21). In an attempt to provide for more interrater reliability, the criticism was, the *DSM-III* had excluded from ASPD diagnosis those individuals who possessed psychopathic traits but who had yet to engage in criminal behavior or had yet to manifest the required conduct disorder. Kiehl and Hoffman describe the situation at the time this way:

> By dropping the affective traits dimension entirely, the DSM-III approach, and its 1987 revisions in DSM-III-R, ended up being both too broad and too narrow. It was too broad because by fixing on behavioral indicators rather than personality it encompassed individuals with completely different personalities, many of whom were not psychopaths. It was also too narrow because it soon became clear that the diagnostic artificiality of this norm-based version of ASPD was missing the core of psychopathy. This seismic definitional change was made in the face of strong criticism from clinicians and academics specializing in the study of psychopathy that, contrary to the framers of the DSM-III, had confidence in the ability of trained clinicians to reliably detect the affective traits. (Kiehl & Hoffman, 2011, p. 365)

By the time work had begun on *DSM-IV*, it had become clear that clinicians had a preference for the trait-centered approach over the behavior-focused approach (Crego & Widiger, 2015). Consequently, the authors of the *DSM-IV* tried to redescribe the criteria for ASPD diagnosis to mirror those present in Hare's PCL-R. A field trial was conducted to compare the relative reliability and validity of the old *DSM-III* criteria and a ten-item set derived from the PCL-R. The results showed that there was a difference in validity depending upon the site in which diagnoses were being made (Widiger et al., 1996). For example, criminal record correlated significantly with both *DSM-III*-defined ASPD and psychopathy in settings like a drug-homelessness clinic and a psychiatric inpatient hospital, but not within the prison setting. Items unique to the PCL-R correlated more highly with *DSM-III*-defined ASPD and psychopathy within the prison setting, but not within clinical settings. Since the *DSM* is designed for use primarily within clinical settings, it was determined that items unique to the PCL-R were not that useful for assessments of psychopathy within mental health settings. Though much of the behaviorally specific requirements from the *DSM-III* were dropped, such as the requirement that "impulsivity or failure to plan ahead" be determined by "traveling from place to place without a prearranged job" or "lack of a fixed address," the criteria for ASPD diagnosis in the *DSM-IV* remained behavior-focused (Crego & Widiger, 2015, p. 669).

The *DSM-V* (2013) included a reclassification of many disorders that shifted numerous individual disorders from one class to another. Although still not an officially recognized clinical diagnosis, with the *DSM-V* psychopathy was, for the first time, included as a "specifier" of ASPD. Crego and Widiger note that since the publication of the *DSM-IV*, considerably more research work had been done regarding psychopathy than for ASPD, and that it appears to them that the original intent of the working groups compiling the *DSM-V* was to define ASPD more in line with the psychopathic personality traits identified by Cleckley and Hare (Crego & Widiger, 2014, 669). The final draft of the *DSM-V*, though it attempted to present a hybrid model for diagnosing ASPD that placed more emphasis on the affective/interpersonal factor of psychopathy than had been present in previous editions of the *DSM*, did not adopt a robust account of psychopathy based on the construct as it was developed by Cleckley and Hare. Instead, Crego and Widiger observe, the *DSM-V* authors relied on a newly developed model of psychopathy developed by Patrick et al. (2009) built around a triarchic model of psychopathy. This triarchic model, assessed via the Triarchic Psychopathy Measure, is built around three core personality traits: boldness, meanness, and disinhibition. In attempt to capture this new model for psychopathy, in the *DSM-V* three additional traits were added under the ASPD diagnosis as potential specifiers for psychopathy: low anxiousness, low social withdrawal, and high attention-seeking (APA, 2013). Still, as only a specific manifestation of ASPD, not a mental disorder unto itself, psychopathy remains to this day an unofficial clinical diagnosis per the *DSM*. Consequently, the relationship between the *DSM* and psychopathy remains "troubled and controversial."

CONCLUSION

Though not a DSM-recognized mental disorder unto itself, psychopathy has for quite some time been treated as such by many psychologists. The intramural squabble over its official recognition aside, the construct of "psychopathy" has achieved firm footing in the academic and clinical literature. The cluster of personality traits at the heart of a "diagnosis" of psychopathy have been much discussed and researched. What makes attributions of psychopathy tricky is the dimensional character of the construct. Most individuals possess at least one of the cluster of psychopathic traits to some degree. Pegging exactly when someone has enough of the personality traits and to a sufficient degree to qualify as a "psychopath" is not an objective science, which is something that critics of the construct often point to. Nonetheless, advocates argue, "psychopathy" is a meaningful psychological construct in that it captures a distinctive type of mental disorder not adequately accounted for by other “official” disorder constructs. For our purposes, the question of the scientific *bona fides* of the construct is not one that needs to be settled. There is sufficient professional support for it to allow the Corporate Psychopath Hypothesis to be taken seriously. We proceed from that position to explicate the details of and support for the Corporate Psychopath Hypothesis in the following chapter.

Chapter Two

Corporate Psychopaths

Seek and Destroy

The term "Corporate Psychopath" was popularized by Boddy in a series of publications in the late 2000s to refer to a subset of psychopathic persons hypothesized to be found in the workplace generally, the corporate environment more specifically, and leadership positions within corporate organizations even more specifically (Babiak and Hare called this group "Snakes in Suits"). Alternatively, this subset of psychopathic persons has been referred to as executive psychopaths, organizational psychopaths, and organizational sociopaths (Pech & Slade, 2007). "Corporate Psychopath" has become the standard reference in the academic literature primarily due to the ongoing work of Boddy and others in generating empirical support for the claim that the category "Corporate Psychopaths" is not just a heuristic device useful in explaining corporate malfeasance and intraorganizational dysfunction, it also has empirical referents in the corporate world and these *actual* "organizational destroyers" can be identified and the harms they cause tracked. Discussion of Corporate Psychopaths has found its way into nonacademic professional publications, some popular magazines, and the news media as well (Hartley, 2016; Wisniewski et al., 2017; Cohan, 2012a; Cohan, 2012b; Tuttle, 2010; Voight, 2012; and Davis, 2017). We will use the designation Corporate Psychopath(s) (Boddy's practice has been to capitalize the reference, which we will follow) throughout the remainder of this text.

So, who is the Corporate Psychopath? Boddy describes their personality this way:

> They are emotionally shallow, calculating and cold, glib and superficially charming, have a grandiose sense of self-worth, are pathological liars, good at conning and manipulating others and have no remorse about harming others;

> they are also callous and lacking in empathy and fail to take responsibility for their own actions. (Boddy, 2014, p. 111)

In essence, "Corporate Psychopaths are simply those psychopaths who work in corporations" (Boddy, 2011b, p. 49). However, as described in the literature, there is one characteristic of Corporate Psychopaths that does mark them off from other groups of psychopathic persons like criminals. They can be described as "successful" or "functional" inasmuch as they have been able to avoid violent behavior as an expression of their psychopathy. They may have hurt others in nonviolent ways, but for some reason they have managed to "channel" their psychopathic needs in ways not requiring violence for satisfaction, and, hence, have managed to not run afoul of the law. Their sense of self-worth is bolstered not by the subordination of others through physical violence but by the power they acquire through their ascension in the corporate world, which affords them the opportunity to subject others to their callous behavior with far less risk of being caught or "outed" due to their charm and the fact that such behavior can be easily written off as part of the price of corporate success. As Babiak and Hare describe it in their preface to *Snakes in Suits*:

> The premise of this book is that psychopaths do work in modern organizations; they often are successful by most standard measures of career success; and their destructive personality characteristics are invisible to most of the people with whom they interact. They are able to circumvent and sometimes hijack succession planning and performance management systems in order to give legitimacy to their behaviors. They take advantage of communication weaknesses, organizational systems and processes, interpersonal conflicts, and general stressors that plague all companies. They abuse coworkers and, by lowering morale and stirring up conflict, the company itself. Some may even steal and defraud. (Babiak & Hare 2006, p. xiv)

As mentioned in the introduction, we will treat the claims that psychopathic persons exist in noticeable numbers in the workforce, specifically the upper reaches of the corporate world, that they cause or have the real potential to cause significant harms to others, the organizations they work for, and the larger social/economic systems in which the organizations they work for are embedded, that they can be identified, and that there exists an ethical obligation to ferret them out (the "search" part) and remove them (the "destroy" part), together, as constituting the Corporate Psychopath Hypothesis.

IN SEARCH OF CORPORATE PSYCHOPATHS

Establishing the existence of Corporate Psychopaths has always been and remains a difficult enterprise. As one would imagine, corporate leaders are not exactly falling over one another to have their employee base, especially their managers, supervisors, directors, and executives, subjected to systematic psychopathy screening. Such screening would require access to employee information, raising privacy concerns. The discovery of Corporate Psychopaths within an organization could create a slew of liability issues connected to employee exposure to harm. And, as will be discussed later in this chapter, corporate leaders may not want their Corporate Psychopaths to be exposed because of the perceived value they bring to the firm. In *Snakes and Suits*, Babiak and Hare summed up the current state of work in establishing the Corporate Psychopath Hypothesis this way:

> Unfortunately, there is no scientific evidence concerning the number of psychopaths in business, for several reasons. First, few organizations will provide the sort of access to their staff and files required to do proper assessments with a standardized instrument, such as the PCL:SV. Second, psychopaths have a talent for hiding their true selves, so one could expect many to go unnoticed and uncounted, leading to an underreporting of psychopathy in business. In the case of particularly successful psychopaths, it may be only the patsies (former pawns) who see behind the masks. Third, psychopathic-like traits and behaviors are also exhibited by some individuals who are not truly psychopathic, which could lead to overreporting, that is, viewing someone as a psychopath when he or she is not. (Babiak & Hare, 2006, p. 177)

Compared to studies involving offender and forensic psychiatric populations, there has been relatively little research regarding psychopathy in the workplace. Most of what does exist is based on small-sample studies, one-off case studies of purported corporate psychopaths, and anecdotal evidence. In *Snakes in Suits*, Babiak and Hare deal almost exclusively with "profiles of generic psychopaths based upon composites of psychopathic characteristics derived from published reports, the news media, and our own research about such personalities" (Babiak p. Hare, 2006, p. xv). The research referenced in this passage is constituted mainly by Babiak's and Hare's experiences over the years interviewing individual psychopathic persons for a range of purposes, supplemented by the study described below. In 2015, Boddy published a longitudinal case study of the CEO of a charitable organization in the UK based on an interview of a senior manager at the charity who had experience with the new CEO and with the new CEO's predecessor (Boddy, 2015b). The interviewee's responses to questions aligned with the PM-MRV indicated that the new CEO embodied all 10 of the characteristics of a Corporate Psychopath.

Limited as it was, Babiak and Hare did much of the early empirical work in establishing the plausibility of the Corporate Psychopath Hypothesis (Babiak, 1995, 2000; Babiak & Hare, 2006). In a few quite constrained instances, clinical or forensic psychologists were able to access corporate personnel for indirect studies of corporate psychopathy by examining the presence of constructs such as narcissism, Machiavelliansim, and self-promotion related to psychopathy (Kets de Vries & Miller, 1984, 2005; Person, 1986). To this date, there have been only three large studies aimed at identifying the presence of Corporate Psychopaths and establishing correlations between their presence and organizational harm, one conducted by Babiak (reported in Babiak and Hare, 2006, and in Babiak, Neumann, and Hare, 2010), and two by Boddy (one reported in Boddy, Ladyshewsky, and Galvin, 2010a, Boddy, Ladyshewsky, and Galvin, 2010b, Boddy, 2011a, and Boddy, 2011b; the second reported in Boddy, 2014). Those three studies will form the empirical basis for the Corporate Psychopath Hypothesis as it is considered here.

The Babiak study, the first of its kind, grew out of several years of consulting work with organizations from which a sample of 203 managers and executives identified for participation in a management development program housed in their respective organizations were selected. Babiak was able to conduct PCL-R assessments on each of the individuals selected for the study. Babiak completed each PCL-R assessment using field notes from face-to-face meetings, observations of social and work-team interactions, and meetings with participants' supervisors, peers, and subordinates (Babiaket al., 2010). These PCL-R scores were converted to PCL:SV equivalents so that the distribution of psychopathic traits in the study subjects could be compared to that found in studies of locality-based populations. This information was supplemented with other information about each individual, such as performance appraisals, including 360-degree evaluations, original resumes, applications, letters of reference, security reports, absenteeism records, and awards. Of the 203 study subjects, 42 held the rank of supervisor or manager, 41 held the rank of director, 51 were vice-presidents, and 21 held the title of CEO, president, or division president. Additionally, 45 nonmanagerial professionals were included in the study because their respective companies had invited them to participate in their management development programs (Babiaket al., 2010, pp. 178–179).

As noted in the previous chapter, PCL-R scores can range from 0–40, with a score of 30 or higher the standard threshold for a "diagnosis" of psychopathy. Babiak's PCL-R assessments of the study participants yielded the following results: 80% of scores fell into the 0-3 range, 4.4% had a score of 25 or higher, and 3.9% had a score of 30 or higher (Babiak et al., 2010). Using the PCL:SV equivalents, for which a score of 13 or higher is generally considered as an indication of "potential" or "possible" psychopathy, 5.9% of the study participants had a score of 13 or higher. This figure compares with a 1.2% rate drawn from general community samples. Further, Babiak reports that 3% of the study sample had a PCL:SV score of 18, compared with a general population rate of .2% (Babiak et al., 2010). As regards possible correlations between study participants' PCL-R scores and the level of executive or management position held, results showed that,

> The PCL-R score was not significantly related to the level of the executive/management position held by a participant . . . Similarly, the PCL-R score was unrelated to whether or not the organization considered a participant to be a high potential candidate. It is important to point out that, of the nine participants with a PCL-R score of 25 or higher, two were vice-presidents, two were directors, two were managers or supervisors, and one held some other management position; thus, they had already achieved considerable rank and status within their respective organizations. (Babiak et al., 2010, p. 185)

This result is important because a key piece of the Corporate Psychopath Hypothesis is that one will find Corporate Psychopaths with greater frequency in senior management levels, and, as we will see, because later studies by Boddy do provide some empirical support for this piece of the Corporate Psychopath Hypothesis.

In general, the study results indicated that mean PCL-R and PCL:SV scores were low in the sample, and that PCL:SV scores were similar to general community sample scores recorded in other studies. The study sample, however, did contain more participants with high PCL:SV scores than are found in general community samples (Babiak et al., 2010). Babiak, Neumann, and Hare, in commenting on some of the more specific findings of the study, which will be discussed later in this chapter, do note that,

> Perhaps the most dramatic results of this study had to do with how the corporation viewed individuals with many psychopathic traits. That is, high psychopathy total scores were associated with perception of good communication skills, strategic thinking, and creative/innovative ability and, at the same time, with poor management style, failure to act as a team player, and poor performance appraisals (as rated by their immediate bosses). These latter associations were rather strong. (Babiak et al., 2010, p. 189)

These results lend empirical credence to that part of the Corporate Psychopath Hypothesis that asserts that, due to their charm and ability to manipulate others, in particular decision-makers in the organizations they inhabit, Corporate Psychopaths are able navigate their way through the job performance and promotion systems they find themselves in without detection.

Boddy has produced the most extensive body of empirical work in support of the Corporate Psychopath Hypothesis. Beginning in 2005 and culminating with his *Corporate Psychopaths: Organizational Destroyers* in 2011, he has crafted the basic arguments for why business organizations and society more broadly should be concerned about the presence of psychopathic persons in positions of leadership in corporate organizations, and conducted empirical research to support the premise that psychopathic persons are a common presence in such leadership positions and are responsible for a range of harms not only within an organization but also to the communities where these organizations are found. As noted earlier, early arguments for this premise tended to be grounded in individual case studies or anecdotal evidence, with Babiak's original study of almost 200 "high-potential executives" representing the only existing, substantive body of empirical support. In 2008, Boddy conducted a study of "a sample of 346 white-collar workers drawn from a variety of professional and managerial associations, members of chambers of commerce, members of charitable organizations, postgraduate business alumni and postgraduate business students and members of other commercial organizations in Australia" (Boddy, Ladyshewsky, and Galvin, 2010a, p. 127). The data for the study was drawn from a self-completed questionnaire distributed to the sample group. The self-completed questionnaire used asked respondents to rate their managers on a variety of behavioral traits. Respondents were allowed to rate both their current managers and managers they had worked with in the past. Questions focused on respondents' experience with managers they would describe as "dysfunctional."

Respondents were asked about the extent to which they had witnessed incidents of bullying and conflict in their workplaces, including experiences of getting into arguments with coworkers, experiences of being yelled at by coworkers, experiences of people being rude at work, and experiences of bullying or unfavorable treatment of others at work (Boddy, 2011b). Relying on previous research indicating that untrained individuals such as work colleagues are capable of identifying psychopathic personality traits in others, Boddy inserted one question in the survey that asked respondents to identify types of behavior found to be indicative of the presence of psychopathic personalities. The behaviors queried about in the questionnaire were ones linked to measures of psychopathy using the PM-MRV. The following table lists the behaviors targeted in the survey and their associated psychopathic personality traits (Boddy, 2011b, p. 14).

Since respondents were allowed to rate both current and previous managers, Boddy received a total of 572 total responses, out of which 487 were used to tabulate results (85 of the responses were incomplete regarding the

Table 2.1.

Behavior	*Psychopathic Personality Trait*
Friendly and extroverted on first meeting; very smooth and persuasive when it suits them	Glib and superficially charming
Able to lie convincingly; able to talk themselves out of trouble	Accomplished liars
Good at using people; well-developed political/networking skills; good at seducing others	Manipulative and conning
Brag about themselves; downplay personal problems; blame others; behave as if above the rules	Grandiose sense of self-worth
Feigning feeling bad about their behavior but not acting as though remorseful; blame others for self-caused troubles; no shame about their ruthlessness in pursuing career at any cost	Lack of remorse about how their actions harm other employees
Not affected by someone close dying or suffering; dramatic displays of emotions that do not look real; claiming friendship with you but unconcerned about your welfare	Emotionally shallow, calculating and cold
Openly make fun of others; selfish and emotionally and verbally abusive of others	Display a lack of empathy; show no capacity to experience the feelings of others
Excuse ready when things go wrong; blame others for own mistakes; claim responsibility for good work of others	Refuse to take responsibility for their own actions

psychopathy scale answers, so they were not included in the study). Using a specialized version of a typical trichotomous categorization used in the study of psychopathic personalities in clinical and forensic settings (i.e., "non-psychopath," "intermediate or moderate psychopaths," and "psychopaths"), Boddy sorted the managers reported on into three groups: "Normal Managers," "Dysfunctional Managers," and "Corporate Psychopaths" (Boddy, 2011b, p. 10). Based on the responses provided to the PM-MRV-linked question in the questionnaire, of the 487 usable responses, Boddy sorted 264 into the Normal Manager category, 104 into the Dysfunctional Manager category, and 119 into the Corporate Psychopath category (Boddy, 2011b, p. 10). This sorting yields a 24% Corporate Psychopath "strike rate" for the sample managers reported on.

In all, the results of the survey were used to explore eight specific hypotheses, which when taken together, make up the Corporate Psychopath Hypothesis:

1. Employees who work in workplaces where managers are perceived to demonstrate the traits associated with being Corporate Psychopaths will report higher levels of conflict at work than those who do not;
2. Employees who work in workplaces where managers are perceived to demonstrate the traits associated with being Corporate Psychopaths will report higher levels of bullying than those who do not;
3. Employees who work in workplaces where managers are perceived to demonstrate the traits associated with being Corporate Psychopaths will report lower levels of workplace corporate social responsibility than those who do not;
4. Employees who work in workplaces where managers are perceived to demonstrate the traits associated with being Corporate Psychopaths will report higher levels of organizational constraints (e.g., conflicting job demands, inadequate training, and inadequate help from others) than those who do not;
5. Employees who work in workplaces where managers are perceived to demonstrate the traits associated with being Corporate Psychopaths will report greater workloads than those who do not;
6. Managers displaying the traits associated with being Corporate Psychopaths will be perceived to be more common at higher levels of management within workplaces than at lower levels;
7. Employees who work in workplaces where managers are perceived to demonstrate the traits associated with being Corporate Psychopaths will report lower levels of job satisfaction than those who do not; and
8. Employees who work in workplaces where managers are perceived to demonstrate the traits associated with being Corporate Psychopaths will report higher levels of withdrawal from the workplace than those who do not. (Boddy, 2011b, pp. 15–18)

Boddy reports that the results of this study supported all eight hypotheses. As he puts it, "[a]s might be expected from the literature, corporate psychopathy correlated significantly with all the constructs under consideration in this research. It can be concluded therefore, that all the variables in this research are related to, and not independent of, the presence of Corporate Psychopaths" (Boddy, 2011b, p. 20).

More specifically, Boddy's study revealed that Corporate Psychopaths appear to be associated with higher levels of management, that respondents occupying more senior positions in firms were more likely to have encountered Corporate Psychopaths, and that those with more work experience also had a higher "contact rate" with Corporate Psychopaths (Boddy, et al., 2010, pp. 128–129). Also, 26% of reported cases of workplace bullying were associated with Corporate Psychopaths (Boddy, 2011a, p. 372), and the reported frequency of unfair supervision was greater in the presence of Corporate Psychopaths (Boddy, 2011a, p. 376).

Boddy argues that his research indicates that the presence of Corporate Psychopaths has six effects on the organizations they inhabit, and a seventh outcome that "magnifies" those six effects. The six effects are,

1. a heightened level of intra-organizational conflict,
2. a dramatic lowering of the perception that the organization behaves in a socially responsible manner and in a way that shows commitment to employees,
3. heavier than necessary organizational constraints in workplaces,
4. higher reports of workplace difficulties due to inadequate training and lack of information about how to perform job responsibilities,
5. negative impacts on reported levels of job satisfaction, and
6. higher levels of withdrawal from work (Boddy, 2011b, pp. 23–25).
7. The magnifying factor is, as noted above, that Corporate Psychopaths are found with greater frequency in higher levels of management: "This gives them the power and influence that magnify their destructive capacity" (Boddy, 2011b, p. 25). This finding is in contrast with that of the Babiak study in that, as noted above, the latter did not find a strong correlation between PCL-R scores and the level of management position held.

The confirmed hypotheses (1), (2), (4), (7), and (8), and the Corporate Psychopath effects (1), (5), and (6) form the basis for the argument that Corporate Psychopaths should be weeded out of the workplace because of the harms they cause to fellow employees within an organization. These confirmed hypotheses and predicted effects of the presence of Corporate Psychopaths combined with confirmed hypothesis (4) and effects (3) and (4) make up the empirical basis for the argument that because they cause harm to the organizations they inhabit, Corporate Psychopaths need to be identified and either kept from gaining employment in organizations or removed from the organizational positions they occupy.

Boddy's second study, conducted in 2011, involved a sample of 304 senior white-collar British managers and professionals selected from a variety of businesses (Boddy, 2014). The study was designed to explore a set of seven hypotheses, similar in nature to those from his earlier Australian study.

Hypothesis 1: Conflict and Bullying are significantly correlated with counterproductive work behavior.
Hypothesis 2: Conflict is higher in the presence of managers who are Corporate Psychopaths.
Hypothesis 3: Bullying is higher in the presence of managers who are Corporate Psychopaths.
Hypothesis 4: Employee affective well-being is lower in the presence of managers who are Corporate Psychopaths.
Hypothesis 5: Employee affective well-being in the presence of managers who are Corporate Psychopaths will be lower among women than among men.
Hypothesis 6: Counterproductive work behavior is higher in the presence of managers who are Corporate Psychopaths.
Hypothesis 7: Counterproductive work behavior in the presence of managers who are Corporate Psychopaths will be lower among women than among men. (Boddy, 2014, pp. 110–111)

The major difference between the two sets of hypotheses is that the latter, those from the 2011 study, included an interest in the differential gender impact of the presence of managers who are Corporate Psychopaths (Hypotheses 5 and 7). The same self-completion questionnaire used in the earlier Australian study was used here as well, and respondents were allowed to report on both current and previous managers. The PM-MRV was built into the questionnaire, as with the Australian study, and used to classify the managers being reported on into the same three groups: Normal Manager, Dysfunctional Manager, and Corporate Psychopath. In total, Boddy received 446 responses. For this study, Boddy reported out the Ns for each group based just on the number of *current* managers respondents commented on (N = 304), not based on the total number of responses received. In particular, Ns for each group were reported in relation to respondents indicating that they had witnessed unfavorable treatment of others or experienced conflict and bullying in the workplace. Of the 304 respondents, based on responses to the PM-MRV question embedded in the questionnaire, 33 had experienced a manager qualifying as a Corporate Psychopath, a percentage of approximately 11% (Boddy, 2014, tables 3 & 4, pp. 114–115). This Corporate Psychopath "strike rate" was less than the 24% reported from the Australian study, but significantly higher than that for the general population nonetheless. A central interest of both studies is the correlation between workplace bullying and the presence of managers who are Corporate Psychopaths. The 2008 Australian study produced the result that 26% of reported incidents of workplace bullying were associated with the presence of Corporate Psychopaths. This second study produced a figure of 35.2% (Boddy, 2014). As for hypotheses five and seven, that one will find differences in the impact of Corporate Psychopaths on men and women regarding employee affective well-being and regarding counterproductive work behavior, they were not born out by the data. The mean scores for men and women in both cases were not significantly different (Boddy, 2014, p. 116).

Boddy draws very similar conclusions from this second study as he does from the earlier one. Corporate Psychopaths are key contributors to low employee affective well-being and to high counterproductive work behavior due to the extent to which they engage in unfair, bullying treatment of others themselves, and allow such behavior to occur in the workforces they manage. As Boddy sums it up, "In terms of affective well-being, when Corporate Psychopaths are present then employees are significantly more likely to feel angry, anxious, bored, depressed and discouraged and significantly less likely to feel at ease, calm or content" (Boddy, 2014, p. 116), all of which leads to higher levels of expressions of counterproductive work behavior. This conclusion is consistent with two effects the presence of Corporate Psychopaths have on employees concluded from his earlier study: namely, that the presence of Corporate Psychopaths in an organization will have a negative impact on employee job satisfaction and will result in higher levels of withdrawal from work. Both studies support the conclusions that higher levels of intraorganizational conflict, in general, are reported in the presence of managers who are Corporate Psychopaths. As indicated above, these findings form the empirical basis for the argument in support of employment screening for psychopathy due to the harm Corporate Psychopaths cause to others in the workplace and in support of the argument that as "destroyers of organizations," Corporate Psychopaths occupying senior management positions should be identified and removed from such positions.

These three studies are the anchor studies for defenders of the Corporate Psychopath Hypothesis. There are other studies, the results of which have been reported out on. In 2005, Board and Fritzon published the results of their study comparing psychopathic personality disorder traits across forensic, psychiatric, and senior business management samples (Board & Fritzon, 2005). Using the dimensional Minnesota Multiphasic Personality Inventory Scales for DSM III Personality Disorders as their measurement instrument, they found that the "emotional components" of psychopathic personality disorder, such as insincerity, superficial charm, egocentricity, grandiosity, and exploitativeness, were significantly present in the senior business manager sample (N = 39) (Board & Fritzon, 2005, p. 25). Jeppesen and Leder ran a study of auditors' experience with Corporate Psychopaths in their client management pool (Jeppesen & Leder, 2016). Based on responses from 179 Danish state-authorized auditors (nine percent of the total population of state-authorized auditors), 69% had experienced Corporate Psychopaths in their client management with 70% having had multiple experiences. Forty-three percent of those auditors with experience with one or more Corporate Psychopaths reported instances of fraud commission associated with their experiences. What is unique about the Jeppesen and Leder study is that it is based on an "outsider's view" of Corporate Psychopaths. The responding auditors are not members of their client organizations, whereas the three anchor studies rely upon reports from individuals who are members of the organizations in which they encounter Corporate Psychopaths. An online survey was used in which respondents were first given descriptions of those psychopathic traits typically associated with psychopathy, then posed a question asking how often they had encountered client managers exhibiting these traits, a question regarding the specific psychopathic traits they had experienced the most in client managers, and whether their experience with these client managers was associated with instances of fraud commission. This study is different from the anchor studies in that no psychiatric assessment tool, like the PCL-R, was used. Instead, the "diagnosis" of psychopathy was based entirely and simply on whether the auditors responding to the online survey self-reported the presence of psychopathic traits in client managers they had worked with in response to a single prompt asking only "In your career as an auditor, have you come across client firms in which managers exhibited psychopathic traits? If yes, how many cases?" (Jeppesen & Leder, 2016, p. 874). Though there is some evidence that "laypersons" are able to reliably identify psychopathic traits in others (see below), relying solely on general, unassessed reports of encounters with psychopathic traits is a weakness of this particular study. Boddy, Miles, Chandana, and Hartog performed a small, qualitative study involving four Human Resources Directors and three other managers in the United Kingdom during the spring and summer of 2013 (Boddy et al., 2015). The four HR Directors had attended a presentation on Corporate Psychopaths prior to be interviewed. Via networking, the three managers were identified as having had experience with Corporate Psychopaths. One-hour interviews were conducted with the seven individuals participating in the study. All but one of the HR Directors reported they had worked with at least one Corporate Psychopath (based on the description of "Corporate Psychopath" they had been introduced to in the presentation prior to their being interviewed) (Boddy et al., 2015, pp. 534–535). The interviewees were given the PM-MRV2 (a shortened version of the PM-MRV) and asked to identify which items from the list they believed applied to the managers they had encountered whom they had identified as potentially Corporate Psychopaths. Their findings were,

> Corporate Psychopaths, at one per cent of the adult population, theoretically exist in all large organizations. This research supports this view because nearly

> all the HR directors involved reported that they thought they had worked with a Corporate Psychopath. Furthermore, all of the six managers nominated by the HR directors as possible psychopaths did score highly enough on our management psychopathy measure to be called Corporate Psychopaths. (Boddy et al., 2015, p. 535)

Authors of all the studies cited recognize that their studies have been limited in size and scope. The populations sampled were not large and they were not randomly selected. This leaves them open to the criticism that they are not truly representative of the overall situation regarding the truth of the Corporate Psychopath Hypothesis. All of the researchers and authors involved in producing and reporting out the results of these three studies acknowledge that this limitation inhibits their ability to generalize from the studied populations to the corporate setting in general, while defending their results as reasonably representative of the general population of corporate managers and executives. There is also the issue of using an instrument to measure the frequency with which psychopathic persons show up in a given population that relies on observational reports of third parties, namely individuals who have come into contact with purported Corporate Psychopaths in the workplace. Boddy's two anchor studies rely entirely on such observational reports, while Babiak's combines information drawn from such reports in the form of performance appraisals, for example, with some direct interviewing. Both rely on research that indicates that psychopathic traits can reliably be observed by untrained individuals who have sufficient experience with the subjects being evaluated (Mahaffey & Marcus, 2006; Fowler & Lilienfeld, 2007). The reliability of using interpersonal reports to measure the frequency of psychopathic personalities remains an unsettled matter. Finally, there is the matter of the reliability and predictive validity of the psychiatric assessment and screening instruments used in the studies (i.e., the PCL-R, the PCL:SV, and the PM-MRV). If these instruments themselves lack sufficient reliability and predictive validity, then the results reported out from the three anchor studies are cast into doubt. The reliability and predictive validity of these assessing and screening instruments will be addressed in chapter four, where the arguments supportive of employment screening for psychopathy are critically evaluated. In terms of allowing the empirical evidence marshalled in support of the Corporate Psychopath Hypothesis to stand for the sake of argument, we will proceed as if the results do meet acceptable standards for empirical research in the social sciences. As regards the arguments for employment screening for psychopathy, they can be made even if there is insufficient evidence to support claims about the particular frequency of Corporate Psychopaths in the workplace (e.g., whether they appear at four to five times the rate of psychopathic personalities in the general population). The argument that organizations should screen for psychopathic personalities is independent of the actual rate at which they appear in business organizations. If there is good reason to believe that Corporate Psychopaths do show up in the workplace and there are good reasons to be concerned about the potential harm they can cause, something there is good evidence to believe, then the actual rate at which they are present is materially irrelevant for arguments supportive of identifying them where they are present and removing them from the workplace *before* they cause harm or cause *more* harm. As we now turn to look at the distinct arguments in support of employment screening for psychopathy, we will rely mainly on the findings from the three anchor studies described above.

THE PREVENTION OF HARM AND UNJUST TREATMENT ARGUMENT

The most frequently referenced argument for identifying Corporate Psychopaths and removing them from the workplace is premised on the claim that they are the perpetrators of harmful and unjust treatment of coworkers, primarily in the form of bullying and related intimidating behavior. This argument is also the one to which most of the empirical research done on the presence of Corporate Psychopaths in the workplace has been directed. There is a larger body of empirical work in the management field that has been conducted on the broader topic of the presence of dark triad personalities (i.e., Machiavellianism, narcissism, and psychopathy) in the workplace, of which research on the presence of psychopathic personalities is a piece. Authors developing this argument have focused their energy on establishing the presence of Corporate Psychopaths and on establishing correlations between their presence and the existence of bullying and intimidating behavior in the specific work environments they are found in. The ethical premise in the argument is assumed by defenders of the Corporate Psychopath Hypothesis.

That ethical premise is this: "Organizations have an obligation to their members to prevent the occurrence of harm whenever and wherever possible." When combined with the empirical premise that Corporate Psychopaths are a common presence in the workplace and they are initiators of harmful and unjust treatment of employees, the argument concludes that organizations have a responsibility to their employees to identify Corporate Psychopaths, where possible, and remove them from the organization. Historically, the ethical premise that employers are obligated to protect employees from harm has, when applied, been focused on concerns related to physical injury or disease incurred while working. The legal case for an employer's obligation to provide for occupational safety is well-established. OSHA and other regulatory bodies in the U.S., and their counterparts in other countries, have the authority to establish and enforce standards for occupational safety, as well as the power to fine employers found to be in violation of promulgated regulations. This in effect creates a legal right to occupational safety and a legal responsibility for employers to provide a workplace free of hazards.

Arguments for an ethical obligation to provide for adequate workplace safety, apart from any legal obligation to do so, typically take one of two basic forms, and have tended to focus on physical injury or disease as well. When present, these arguments would cover any physical injury that Corporate Psychopaths may cause. As will be seen later in this section, the harms that Corporate Psychopaths are claimed to be responsible for are primarily of the psychological or emotional variety, though declines in physical health can indirectly result from the infliction of the psychological and emotional suffering Corporate Psychopaths are believed to be more directly responsible for causing. For example, Han, Harms, and Bai have shown that "abusive supervision," which would include the kinds of behavior that Corporate Psychopaths engage in via their supervisory roles, leads to declines in worker creativity *via* the mediating effects of sleep deprivation and emotional exhaustion created by the abusive supervision (Han et al., 2017). These arguments, however, can be easily extended to cover the losses in psychological and emotional well-being that employees endure as a result of working in the presence of Corporate Psychopaths. The psychic pains suffered by victims of workplace sexual and racial harassment and discrimination are readily acknowledged by the law and ethics as undeserved and unjust harms. The same could be said for the pains caused by abusive supervision at the hands of Corporate Psychopaths. Therefore, the prevention of harm and unjust treatment argument for Corporate Psychopath screening can easily rely on ethical arguments for employee occupational safety.

The first basic form of the argument for a duty to provide for a safe workplace is grounded in the premise that employees have an inherent, moral right to occupational safety. The employer's duty to provide for that safety is demanded by the possession of the right by employees. This claim is not, however, accepted by all strands of moral and political philosophy. Libertarians, like Tibor Machan, have rejected the claim that individuals have any specific moral rights beyond the basic rights to life, liberty, and property that are held by all persons (Machan, 1987). A right to occupational safety would be considered a specific right since it is attributed to a specific group of persons, in this case employees. Any specific rights that individuals may acquire are the result of legislative action or the product of some contract or agreement between themselves and others. In either case, the specific rights in question are not *moral* rights. Further, the libertarian argument goes, assigning to any individual or group of individuals rights that are positive in nature, rights that require that others act so as to satisfy the claim embodied in the positive right, is to impinge upon the liberty of others. The right to occupational safety would be such a positive right because, if acknowledged or granted, it places upon employers the duty to provide for a safe workplace. According to this line of thought, the basic moral rights that individuals do possess, to life, liberty, and property, are negative rights in that they only require others to refrain from acting in ways to deny either of the three. They don't stand as restrictions on the liberty of others.

The argument that, indeed, individuals do possess some inherent moral rights is most often based on one of two considerations about the nature of being human. The first, what has come to be known as the "interests theory approach," argues that a defining feature of being human is the possession of interests, some of which are common to all humans because their satisfaction or lack of satisfaction impact human well-being in essential ways. If we are to respect human beings, acknowledge their dignity as persons, then we must recognize that they have basic rights to have those essential interests satisfied. Our interests matter to us, as the interests of others matter to them as well. For each of us to protect our own interests and our pursuit of their satisfaction requires that others refrain from unjustifiably interfering with that pursuit and, when the conditions are right, act so that those interests are not threatened. From this perspective, to speak of "moral rights" is to refer to those expectations that are part of the systems of cooperation that we adopt as we go about leading our lives as interest-bearing beings. The second consideration often used to ground a claim about the existence of moral rights is that human beings are purposive agents capable of setting for ourselves the ends that we seek to pursue in life and mapping out how we would prefer to go about attaining those ends. This approach is often referred to as the "will theory approach." We are, to put it succinctly in Kantian terminology, rational autonomous beings, end-in-ourselves. As we desire to have ourselves treated as such, we recognize that all other rational autonomous beings desire the same thing. To speak of "moral rights" is to refer to those expectations that all purposive agents can rationally have of others regarding how they are treated because of the nature of their being. Put in a more strictly Kantian way, rational autonomous beings understand that they have a duty to "act in such a way that you treat humanity, whether in your own person or in the person of any other, never merely as a means to an end, but always at the same time as an end" (Kant, *Grounding for the Metaphysics of Morals*). For both approaches, the right to be free from harm and injury is expressive of an essential human interest and necessary to continued functioning as a purposive agent.

The second basic form of the argument for a right to occupational safety is contractarian in nature. Under this form, all rights are treated as "civil" rights in the sense that they are granted to individuals by the society they live in, not possessed inherently by human beings. A similar position is taken regarding duties. Drawing upon the classical social contract philosophies of Hobbes and Locke, this approach to the question of moral rights explores which liberties and protections humans would opt to have as part of their social contract given that, in principle, they were forfeiting unlimited liberty to live socially. The liberties retained and the protections gained must, on balance, offset that forfeiture of unlimited liberty. Of course, it would be rational to demand that one have protection against murder and serious bodily harm as part of the social contract. To ensure that such protection is taken seriously, members of society are granted the right to not suffer in those ways. The task of contractarian thinking in general is to delineate which rights would necessarily need to be part of the social contract. An enduring problem of the contractarian approach is how to describe the status of individuals as they agree to the tenets of the social contract. Recognizing that if original contractors are making their decisions to opt in or not based on the actual positions they find themselves in as they contemplate consent, there is little likelihood that a contract can actually be reached as each party to the social contract would want it shaped in ways that benefit them uniquely in terms of the specific interests they have. Contemporary contractarian thinking, originating with Rawls in the 1970s, treats the social contract as "hypothetical" agreement in the sense that it is not a document that discrete individuals actually create. Instead, it treats the original contractors as idealized persons choosing in ignorance of their own particular stake in the content of the social contract, a heuristic device Rawls described as choosing from behind "the veil of ignorance" in the "original position." The question, then, becomes what constellation of liberties and protections would any rational, self-interested, yet ignorant, contractor seek out? Rawls argued that one of the basic rights that would find expression in the social contract would be the "freedom of the person, which includes freedom from psychological oppression and physical assault and dismemberment (integrity of the person)" (Rawls, 1999, p. 53). In their application of Rawlsian social contract thinking to business ethics, Donaldson and Dunfee argue that one of the basic norms of the social contract (what they refer to collectively as "hypernorms") would be a norm "requiring feasible workplace safety practices essential to protect against serious physical injury" (Donaldson & Dunfee, 1999, p. 62). As noted above, this line of argumentation could easily be extended to cover psychological and emotional injury.

Obviously, moral and political philosophers continue to debate the bases of rights claims. That there are well-argued for theories of moral rights is sufficient for the prevention of harm and unjust treatment argument for Corporate Psychopath screening. Even if no persuasive argument for the existence of a moral right to occupational safety is available, the undisputed existence of a legal right to occupational safety would suffice to create a duty on behalf of employers to prevent workplace harm and injury from occurring where possible. We now turn to the other premise of the prevention of harm and unjust treatment argument, namely the claim that Corporate Psychopaths pose a substantial risk of causing harm and injury in the workplace.

In his research, alone and with colleagues, Boddy has focused on three types of harms that Corporate Psychopaths cause: (1) bullying (either engaging in it themselves or fostering an environment conducive to it), (2) the creation of conditions in the workplace that lead to counterproductive work behavior, and (3) behaving in ways that have a negative impact on employee affective well-being. In all three cases, the harm created for coworkers by Corporate Psychopaths is not deserved. We will consider the first and third types of harm in this section as they are harms done to coworkers whereas the second type of harm, the creation of conditions fostering counterproductive work behavior, will be discussed in the next section since it has primarily to do with harm to the organization.

Boddy works with the following definition of "workplace bullying," drawn from research on the subject: "Workplace bullying is defined as the repeated unethical and unfavorable treatment of one person by another in the workplace" (Boddy, 2011a, p. 367). Workplace bullying can take on a number of different forms. It can involve direct acts of intimidation and abuse, such as public behavior intended to belittle and humiliate others, including verbal sarcasm and name calling, the scapegoating of others, or the application of undeserved work pressure. It can also involve more subtle forms such as gossiping and social exclusion in the workplace. In their 2018 summary of existing research on workplace bullying, Nielsen and Einarsen note that, when compared to other forms of "psychological aggression" in the workplace,

> . . . the definitional characteristics of workplace bullying clearly highlights bullying as a unique, and especially detrimental, form of aggression at the workplace. Some forms of workplace aggression, such as incivility and social undermining, is defined as deviant, but low in intensity and happening infrequently and occasionally, typically involving behavior with ambiguous intent to harm the target. Workplace bullying, however, is defined as situations where an employee repeatedly and over a prolonged time period is exposed to harassing behavior from one or more colleagues (including subordinates and leaders) and where the targeted person is unable to defend him/herself against this systematic mistreatment. (Nielsen & Einarsen, 2018, p. 73)

Drawing upon existing literature, they highlight three defining features of workplace bullying: (1) it involves systematic negative and unwanted social behavior in the workplace, (2) it occurs over an extended period of time, and (3) the target cannot easily avoid or act so as to put an end to the unwanted behavior (Nielsen & Einarsen, 2018).

The hypothesis that workplace bullying would positively correlate with the presence of Corporate Psychopaths has intuitive bite to it inasmuch as many of the defining personality traits of individuals described as bullies are found with equal measure in psychopathic individuals. As Boddy notes, "[t]he traits of narcissism, lack of self-regulation, lack of remorse, and lack of conscience have been identified as those displayed by bullies. These traits are shared with psychopathy indicating there is some theoretical cross-over between bullies and psychopaths" (Boddy, 2011a, p. 368). Some research has shown that individuals scoring highly on a psychopathic measure are more likely to engage in bullying (Nathanson et al., 2006). Babiak and Hare have also reported that a significant portion of the Corporate Psychopaths they identified in their anchor study (two of seven) were also bullies (Babiak & Hare, 2006). Not surprisingly since it has always been a main focus of his research, Boddy's two anchor studies provide the most substantial body of empirical evidence for a link between workplace bullying, and other forms of intimidating behavior, and the presence of Corporate Psychopaths. In his first study, the sample of Australian senior white-collar workers, Boddy found that 26% of all reported cases of witnessing of bullying were associated with the presence of Corporate Pscyhopaths (Boddy, 2011a and 2011b). Additionally, Boddy's analysis of the results of this respondent sample indicated that there was a "very strong and significant correlation coefficient in a positive direction" between the presence of Corporate Psychopaths and the frequency of bullying reported. As the presence of Corporate Psychopaths in a work environment increases, so does the level of bullying reported (Boddy, 2011a). Based on the respondent sample, the average frequency of reported incidents of bullying per year at work in organizations where Corporate Psychopaths were not present was 9.0 (less than an incident per month) while that for organizations where Corporate Psychopaths were present was 64.4 (more than an incident per week) (Boddy, 2011b). In addition to measuring the correlation between workplace bullying and the presence of Corporate Psychopaths, Boddy's Australian study also asked respondents about the frequency of their witnessing other unfair treatment of employees. He found that 17.6% of reported cases of getting into arguments with others at work, 22.8% of reported cases of people yelling at respondents at work, and 25.1% of cases of people being rude to respondent at work occurred in the presence of Corporate Psychopaths (Boddy, 2011b). More telling, the percentage of respondents who reported having experienced each of these types of treatment was higher in all cases in the presence of Corporate Psychopaths than it was for the other two scenarios (i.e., in the presence of Normal Managers or in the presence of Dysfunctional Managers) as judged by the responses to the PM-MRV question embedded in the survey questionnaire (Boddy, 2011b).

Why do Corporate Psychopaths engage in workplace bullying themselves or act so as to create the conditions for it to occur amongst their coworkers? For Corporate Psychopaths, as is the case for psychopathic personalities in general, bullying is one way of satisfying a desire to hurt people, a desire that is quite common in psychopathic personalities, even if only for the amusement that it brings (Clarke, 2007). Bullies tend to display a lack of self-regulation, remorse, and conscience, traits that are also find in heightened ways in psychopathic personalities. In a sense, bullying behavior is a "natural" outgrowth of the Corporate Psychopath personality. But, for Corporate Psychopaths, bullying also has utilitarian value. In addition to the role that bullying plays in intimidating coworkers so that they do not challenge them, Clarke has noted that Corporate Psychopaths often use bullying to distract attention away from their other behaviors that if noticed by coworkers, would threaten their continued organizational existence or interfere with their attempts to progress within the organization (Clarke, 2005).

Drawing upon the results from two meta-analyses of the existing literature on the potential effects of bullying, Nielsen and Einarsen note that "[t]he findings show that exposure to bullying is associated with both job-related and health- and well-being-related outcomes, such as mental and physical health problems, symptoms of post-traumatic stress, burnout, increased intentions to leave, and reduced job satisfaction and organizational commitment" (Nielsen & Einarsen, 2012, p. 309). Further evidence of the negative effects of bullying on the psychological health of victims can be found in a yearlong study of 500 Australian employees that found that being subjected to workplace bullying led to health impairment and lower worker engagement resulting in increased absenteeism (Magee et al., 2017).

Bullying behavior in the workplace is known to beget further workplace bullying. It has been recognized since the 1990s that a stressful working environment can lead to bullying (e.g., Leymann, 1996; Van den Brande, et al., 2016). Grounded in social learning theory, which posits that much of human behavior is learned through observation of the behavior of others, research has emerged documenting the extent to which individuals in the workplace who experience bullying themselves come to emulate that behavior themselves, especially if the experience of being bullied is accompanied by an observation that benefits appear to attach to the bullying of others (e.g., promotions, raises, etc.) (Folger & Skarlicki, 1998; Robinson & O'Leary-Kelley,

1998; Lee & Brotheridge, 2006). In a large study of over two thousand members of the Norwegian workforce, Hauge, Skogstad, and Einarsen found that "being oneself a target of bullying, regardless of the frequency, and being male *[research indicates that males engage in workplace bullying more often than females]* strongly predicted involvement of bullying of others" (Hauge et al., 2009, p. 349) (italicized addition mine). Additionally, research indicates that some employees subject to abusive, unfair supervision in the workplace initiate similar behavior themselves as a way to find relief from the negative emotional states they find themselves in as a result of having been subjected to abusive behavior; in effect bullying, for some, functions as an "emotional pressure relief valve" (Folger & Skarlicki, 1998; Andersson & Pearson, 1999). This is not to say that all victims of abusive supervision will become workplace bullies themselves. Some are able to endure ongoing abusive supervision without resorting to the same behavior in retaliation or as a psychological release. McCallister and Perrewe have argued that an abused employee's ability to resist engaging in the same behavior is tied to their store of self-regulating capacity, where "self-regulation" is understood to mean, "the capacity for altering one's own responses, especially to bring them into line with standards such as ideals, values, morals, and social expectations, and to support the pursuit of long-term goals" (McAllister & Perrewe, 2018, p. 878, quoting Baumeister et al., 2007). This self-regulatory capacity can be diminished over time as it is repeatedly drawn upon to resist responding to bullying with bullying (directed either at the initiator of the bullying, or more likely on an unsuspecting third party). Consequently, even though it is not the case that all victims of workplace bullying will respond in kind, the impact on their ability to restrain themselves is threatened by the presence of Corporate Psychopaths.

In summary, then, if there is evidence that the presence of Corporate Psychopaths in the workplace correlates with frequency of bullying behavior, and other forms of intimidation, then employees' right to occupational safety entails that organizations are responsible for creating a work environment where employees are not subjected to the range of psychological and emotional harms that the presence of Corporate Psychopaths gives rise to. Notice that this obligation is a preventive one. It requires that the workplace be safe, be free of the risk of harm, whether any such harm has actually happened.

THE REDUCTION OF ORGANIZATIONAL RISK ARGUMENT

The infliction of harmful and unjust treatment by Corporate Psychopaths also poses a risk to the organizations in which they reside. Organizations in which Corporate Psychopaths reside bear legal and moral liability for the harms caused to coworkers by Corporate Psychopaths in their employ. This liability creates, at the least, financial risk if not complete ruin. The punitive and restorative costs of lawsuits and regulatory fines create serious financial risk for such organizations. However, the organizational risks that accompany the employ of Corporate Psychopaths go beyond the direct financial risks associated with the liability for preventing harm. Given their single-minded pursuit of their own personal aggrandizement, Corporate Psychopaths can be expected to make entirely self-centered decisions with little or no regard for their impact on the well-being of the organizations they work for. Defenders of the Corporate Psychopath Hypothesis have cited these other organizational risks as grounds for employment screening for psychopathy. The organizational risks cited include the potential damage to organizational reputation, internally and externally, the potential for fraudulent behavior, and the need to incur substantial costs to implement organizational constraints aimed at preventing or ameliorating the effects of counterproductive work behavior triggered by the presence of Corporate Psychopaths in positions of power. We consider this organizational risk argument in this section.

The organizational risk argument is grounded in one or both of two ethical claims: (1) managers of business organizations have a duty to act so as to minimize the risks to their organizations that accompany their legitimate business operation, and (2) business owners have a right to expect that the duties embedded in the principal-agent relationship they have with managers are met by those agents. The two claims are clearly related, in fact one could argue that the managerial duty to defend the business is derived from the principal-agent relationship they are a part of. But, the managerial duty to defend isn't necessarily only found in a principal-agent relationship. One's duty to defend their family from harm isn't based on a principal-agent relationship. So, we can treat the two as separate, grounding, ethical claims.

The moral duty to defend the organization one works for from risk or harm is a "role duty" and the duties involved are "special obligations." Managers have the duty because of the particulars of their role as managers. It is quite common, and reasonable, for us to believe that we have various special obligations to those to whom we stand in some sort of special relationship, like friends, family, professional colleagues, those to whom we have made promises or commitments of some sort, and, we might add, organizations that employ us. For the last, special obligations to the organizations we work for, they can be understood as examples of what moral philosophers more generally call "promissory obligations" or "contractual obligations." Employees of an organization, in particular managers, have made a "promise" or "contracted" to act in the best interest of the firms they work for, unless doing so would require them to violate the rights of others, fail to perform other weightier duties they possess, or have their own rights violated due to coercive pressure to fulfill their duty to the firm. Though not uncontroversial, it can be argued that the employment contract carries with it, even if only implicitly, a duty to not only avoid directly harming the firm but also the duty to defend it against harm where possible and reasonably prudent to do so. Again, this more expansive, "positive duty" to act so as to defend the organization against harm (the duty to not cause harm is a "negative duty" inasmuch as it requires the duty-holder to not do something) can be understood as a "promissory" or "contractual" duty attached to one's employment contract. Legally, the duty to keep from harm can be understood to be an example of a fiduciary duty, in most cases grounded in a legally recognized principal-agent relationship. This duty is codified in corporate law as expressly applying to executives and directors of corporations.

Citing the work of Quinn and Jones (Quinn & Jones, 1995), Boddy frames the threat that Corporate Psychopaths pose to their principal-agent relationship with the organizations that employ them in this way:

> In terms of the moral duty that [these] managers have towards the organization that employs them, commentators have argued that the principal-agent model of the organization requires that managers develop their business policies with reference to certain moral duties . . . managers who are Corporate Psychopaths have no conscience or sense of morality at all. They are thought to seek self-gratification and self-enrichment rather than work towards the benefit of an organization, and this self-seeking behavior can be expected to jeopardise organizational productivity and effectiveness and to increase constraints within an organization. (Boddy, 2011b, p. 78)

Based in a consideration of the moral implications of agency theory, Quinn and Jones argue that whatever additional duties managers may acquire because of their status as agents of a business's owners, they are bound by a set of four more basic moral duties, the acceptance of which is necessary for the principal-agent relationship to exist in the first place. The four basic moral duties are: (1) avoiding harm to others, (2) respecting the autonomy of others, (3) avoiding lying, and (4) honoring agreements (Quinn & Jones, 1995). The implication is that, "[i]f we accept that managers have a moral duty to maximize the wealth of shareholders, we must also logically accept the following: managers must settle on business policies that do not contravene the four moral principles upon which economic activity and agency relationships are founded" (Quinn & Jones, 1995, p. 36). Since Corporate Psychopaths are incapable of conceiving of such moral duties, they are bound to "settle" on business policies within their control that serve only their narrow self-interest and that threaten the well-being of the organization itself. Therefore, non-psychopathic managers and executives are morally bound to protect their firms from the harms psychopathic personalities in their midst can cause as a function of preserving not just the legal requirements of their principal-agent relationship with the firm's owners, but also to satisfy the moral duties they are bound by as part of the necessary conditions for the existence of that relationship.

As described above, Boddy's Australian study yielded the general result that conflict in the workplace and the presence of Corporate Psychopaths are positively correlated. As the presence of Corporate Psychopaths increases, so do reports of workplace conflicts, such as experiences of being involved in argument, being yelled at, being treated rudely, and being the target of bullying. Such conflicts create direct harms to employees in the form of emotional suffering, diminished self-esteem, decreased job satisfaction, and other kinds of mental health problems. The unjustified harms suffered by victims of the behavior of Corporate Psychopaths also have a spillover effect on organizational "health." Bruk-Lee and Spector have reported empirical evidence that experiencing negative emotions at work due to workplace stress and conflict is positively correlated with counterproductive workplace behavior (Bruk-Lee & Spector, 2006). Clarke has described the impact that the behavior of Corporate Psychopaths has on the emotional states of coworkers (Clarke, 2007). The bullying and intimidating behaviors that characterize the manner in which Corporate Psychopaths conduct themselves in the workplace in pursuit of their own gain causes the targets of their behavior to experience anger, fear, sadness, anxiety, embarrassment, guilt, depression, and confusion, all of which, Clarke argues, decreases employee effectiveness and productivity and leads to an increase in the range and extent of organizational constraints that employers must put in place. Boddy's research, as presented above, has also confirmed the hypothesis that in the presence of Corporate Psychopaths, employees will experience higher levels of organizational constraints where such constraints are understood to be "situations or things in the place of employment which interfere with the efficient performance of a task at work" such as poor equipment or supplies, excessive organizational rules and procedures, interruption by others, and inadequate help from others (Boddy, 2011b, pp. 79–80). The correlation is linear, as the presence of Corporate Psychopaths increases so do the organizational constraints employees experience, which cause increased difficulty in carrying out their job functions on a daily basis. These constraints negatively impact the operational efficiency of firms where they are present in significant numbers and amounts, and also lead to lower worker productivity. The need for or presence of more and more organizational constraints due to Corporate Psychopaths in the workplace creates a risk factor for firms that they must address at cost.

Counterproductive work behavior, the research previously described shows, is another byproduct of the presence of Corporate Psychopaths in the workplace. In his study of British white-collar employees, Boddy hypothesized that "counterproductive work behavior is higher in the presence of managers who are Corporate Psychopaths" (Boddy, 2014, p. 111). By "counterproductive work behavior," Boddy means the deliberate jeopardizing of workplace outcomes and normal functioning and "has well-established connections with productivity and efficiency" (Boddy, 2014, p. 109). Examples include the seeking of revenge on perceived perpetrators of workplace conflict, sabotaging of coworkers, misuses of time and business resources, intentionally performing work incorrectly, and purposely failing to follow directions. The hypothesis that counterproductive work behavior would be found to be higher in the presence of managers who are Corporate Psychopaths was supported by Boddy's study.

In addition to possible links to active counterproductive work behavior, there is evidence that the subjects of workplace bullying adopt absenteeism as an avoidance response to bullying, what we might call passive counterproductive work behavior as rates of employee absenteeism correlate with loss of worker productivity within an organization. Analyzing the results of the European Working Conditions Surveys of 2000, 2005, and 2010, which consisted of over 33,000 interviews with employees from the 15 EU countries at the time, Martin and Matiaske report that across all three survey years, on average, 9% of female respondents and 7% of male respondents reported having been the subject of intimidating or bullying behavior (Martin & Matiaske, 2017). Regarding employee absenteeism, Martin and Matiaske reported that "the likelihood for the occurrence of work-related absence from work climbs two- to threefold when social stressors in the form of harmful behavior occur" (Martin & Matiaske, 2017, p. 240). "Harmful behavior" includes but is not restricted to intimidation or bullying; it also includes discrimination and physical violence, but in the survey results workers reported being the subject of intimidation or bullying at a rate two to three times higher than they reported being the subject of other types of harmful behavior. Their analysis, nonetheless, indicated that "Intimidation in the workplace causes the percentage of absentee behavior of employees to increase by 6.3%—as compared to workplaces where intimidation does not occur, it may even increase by twice that amount or 12.6%" (Martin & Matiaske, 2017, p. 245). As noted above, Magee et al.'s study of the effects of workplace bullying on Australian workers indicated that the presence of workplace bullying led to increased absenteeism and, subsequently, a loss in workplace productivity (Magee et al., 2017). However, not all studies show that exposure to workplace bullying is positively associated with increased rates of absenteeism. Nielsen and Einarsen conclude that a meta-analytic review of existing literature on the effects of workplace bullying on individual employees does not establish a strong association between the two (Nielsen & Einarsen, 2012).

Some research also shows that lower levels of job satisfaction are correlated with abusive supervision of employees. Defining “abusive supervision” to mean “the sustained display of hostile verbal and nonverbal behaviors, excluding physical contact,” Tepper has shown that employees subject to such supervisory experiences not only express lower levels of job satisfaction, but they also report negative impacts on their overall life satisfaction sufficient to cause them to quit their jobs (Tepper, 2000). Boddy’s research supports this finding (Boddy, 2006, 2011b, 2014) as well as research by Stringer (Stringer, 2006) and Lapierre, Spector, and Leck (Lapierre et al., 2005). Kahn’s work has shown that employees who experience a low-quality relationship with their supervisors, an experience that coworkers of Corporate Psychopaths would have, are more likely to strive for bare minimal levels of productivity which makes it more likely they will feel lower levels of job satisfaction leading to increased levels of burnout, absenteeism, and turnover (Kahn, 1998). Given its documented negative impact on employee productivity, and the additional costs to the firm (e.g., the recruitment costs associated with high levels of employee turnover), employee job satisfaction is something that a firm has a strong interest in maintaining. The presence of Corporate Psychopaths poses a risk to the satisfaction of this business interest.

In line with the narcissistic component of their personality type, it can be presumed that Corporate Psychopaths would exhibit little concern and care for the health of the firms they work for. To the extent that they would exhibit such care in their behavior and decision-making, it would be only to the extent that doing so directly benefits them. Because of this, a part of the Corporate Psychopath Hypothesis is that organizations that employ Corporate Psychopaths would experience a higher rate of business failure than those that do not. Boddy admits in his 2015 review of the past decade of work on the Corporate Psychopath Hypothesis that, “There has been no direct empirical evidence linking corporate failure with the presence of psychopaths” (Boddy, 2015a, p. 2413). Individual case studies such as the collapse of Enron and that of the UK newspaper the *Daily Mirror* are cited as examples of corporate failure due to the actions of Corporate Psychopaths, Kenneth Lay and Robert Maxwell respectively, who, Boddy asserts, score high on psychopathy measures based on their known behavior leading to the collapse of the firms they led (Boddy, 2015a). As noted above, Jeppesen and Leder’s study of Danish auditors and their experience with client managers indicated that a high number of auditors had experienced behavior typical of Corporate Psychopaths (69%) and that 43% of that group had detected fraud in their professional experience with those managers (Jeppessen & Leder, 2016). The commission of fraud, of course, threatens the financial health and future of firms. This supports the hypothesis that firms with psychopathic personalities in positions of significant financial decision-making power are at higher risk of business failure.

As with the prevention of harm and unjust treatment argument, the conclusion here is that there are legal and moral grounds for organizations to engage in employment screening for psychopathy. Unlike the previous argument, here the legal and moral ground is that organizations have a right to protect themselves from the various risks to organizational health that the presence of Corporate Psychopaths poses, rather than a duty to protect others. This right, however, does give rise to the managerial duty to defend the firm, a duty that can be added to the managerial duty to prevent harm to and unjust treatment of their subordinates.

THE PROTECTION OF ECONOMIC/SOCIAL SYSTEMS ARGUMENT

Early in the academic discussion of the Corporate Psychopath Hypothesis, Boddy suggested that stakeholder groups external to the organization, in this case pension funds, would have a legitimate interest in whether organizations they invest in, or may potentially invest in, screen for psychopathy as a way of minimizing their risk (Boddy, 2006). Given the evidence cited above that Corporate Psychopaths are willing to engage in fraudulent behavior that creates serious risks for the organizations that employ them, it is reasonable for third parties like pension funds and, for that matter, any other party or organization whose own financial health can be impacted by the decisions Corporate Psychopaths make, to make ethical claims that firms should invest in management measures aimed at reducing this indirect harm via psychopathy screening. We generally hold individuals and organizations legally and ethically responsible for the indirect harm their actions cause if such harms are foreseeable and can with reasonable effort be avoided. Legally, "vicarious liability" is recognized as the liability that a supervisory party, such as an employer, has for the actions of subordinates, such as employees, which, in the course of the performance of their work, harm others. A common type of legal vicarious liability is exhibited in cases of workplace discrimination or harassment. From an ethical perspective, May has argued for a similar type of organizational responsibility based on the idea of "vicarious agency" (May, 1983). In addressing the question of corporate responsibility, May argued for the view that corporations can only act "vicariously" through the actual behaviors of their agents. They are not, as French had argued, intentional agents in their own right (French, 1979). Even though they are only vicarious agents, May argues that corporations can still be held morally responsible for the actions of the agents through which they are said to "act." He grounds that responsibility in the claim that corporations can be "vicariously negligent."

A corporation is vicariously negligent for the harmful acts of one of its members if:

(a) *causal factor*—the member of the corporation was enabled or facilitated in his or her harmful conduct by the general grant of authority given to him or her by corporate decision; and
(b) *fault factor*—appropriate members of the corporation failed to take preventative measures to thwart the potential harm by those who could harm due to the above general grant of authority, even though:
    1. the appropriate members could have taken such precautions, and
    2. these appropriate members could reasonably have predicted that the harm would occur. (May, 1983, p. 78)

The crux of the Corporate Psychopath Hypothesis is that Corporate Psychopaths are able to cause the harm they cause, or have the potential to cause harm, because of the power they acquire within the corporations. That power is a function of the "grant of authority" they are given by their superiors. It is also part of the Corporate Psychopath Hypothesis that, in many if not most cases, attentive managers and HR professionals within an organization could identify the Corporate Psychopaths in their midst and could "reasonably have predicted that harm would occur" from their presence. May's account of vicarious negligence provides a basis for arguing that organizations can be held morally responsible for the harm caused by the Corporate Psychopaths they employ to the larger economic and social systems in which they operate.

Boddy and others have extended the argument that third parties have a legitimate ethical expectation that organizations they are linked to in stakeholder relationships take steps to reduce the risk that employing Corporate Psychopaths create to a broader argument that Corporate Psychopaths pose a threat to the financial well-being of the larger economic and social systems in which organizations are located. In particular, the 2007–2008 global financial crisis is targeted by these authors as the result, whole or in part, of the presence of Corporate Psychopaths in those financial corporations at the heart of the crisis. When first broached by Boddy in his "The Corporate Psychopaths Theory of the Global Financial Crisis," the connection between the presence of Corporate Psychopaths in upper-level positions in global financial institutions and the events leading to the Global Financial Crisis of the late 2000s was couched in very speculative terms (Boddy, 2011c). Acknowledging that it is just a *theory*, he describes it this way:

> The Corporate Psychopaths Theory of the Global Financial Crisis is that Corporate Psychopaths, rising to key senior positions within modern financial corporations, where they are able to influence the moral climate of the whole organization and wield considerable power, have largely caused the crisis. In these senior corporate positions, the Corporate Psychopath's single-minded pursuit of their own self-enrichment and self-aggrandizement to the exclusion of all other considerations has led to an abandonment of the old fashioned concept of *noblese oblige*, equality, fairness, or of any real notion of corporate social responsibility. (Boddy, 2011c, p. 257)

He remarks at the end of this "short theoretical paper" that "[w]hen presented to management academics in discussion, the Corporate Psychopaths Theory of the Global Financial Crisis is accepted as being plausible and highly relevant," and that the theory is one "that would benefit from further development and research" (Boddy, 2011c, p. 258). By 2016, in his review of the work done on the Corporate Psychopath Hypothesis during the decade ending in 2015, Boddy flat out declares that, "Financial insiders as well as psychologists and management researchers agree that corporate psychopaths within banks were linked to the global financial crisis" (Boddy, 2015a, p. 2412). Unfortunately, the citations he provides in support of this claim are to his own work, directly or indirectly. Considering this to be supporting evidence for the Psychopaths Theory, Boddy cites research by Andrews that indicated psychopathy scores are higher among finance students than they are among other students (Andrews, 2015).

This argument for psychopathy screening is the weakest of those presented in the literature. It entirely lacks empirical support, though as Boddy remarked, it is a "plausible" theory. Its plausibility is grounded in the available empirical research that does indicate that behavior based in greed, avarice, and an absence of conscience was at the heart of the financial practices that precipitated the Global Financial Crisis, behavior that is typical of psychopathic personalities. That the actual individuals involved in those practices are Corporate Psychopaths cannot be established as there has never been an opportunity to screen them for psychopathy. Though a good inference it may be, the Corporate Psychopath Theory of the Global Financial Crisis remains just that, an inference. Nonetheless, it has been offered as a reason for engaging in employment screening for psychopathy, and it has caught the attention of authors in the popular media (e.g., Cohan 2012b and Ritholtz, 2012). For these reasons, it is included here.

THE POSITIVE BUSINESS INTEREST ARGUMENT

The title of this chapter captures the fact that the Corporate Psychopath Hypothesis calls not just for the identification of Corporate Psychopaths (the "seek" part), but also for their ouster from the workplace (the "destroy" part). This is because the most relied upon arguments for employment psychopathy screening, described above, are grounded in the negative impact of Corporate Psychopaths on organizations. Their presence, it is argued, leads to the harmful and unjust treatment of coworkers, creates prominent risks to the "health" of organizations, and threatens to destabilize the larger social/economic systems that are the context in which the organizations that employ them operate and receive their sanction to do so. Business organizations have a responsibility to prevent those things from happening, and hence have a legitimate business interest in preventing the hiring of psychopathic personalities as well as in identifying and removing those already in their midst. These arguments support the normative portion of the Corporate Psychopath Hypothesis.

Paradoxically, an argument has been advanced that, contrary to the negative public wrap they have gotten over the past two decades, Corporate Psychopaths may, in certain situations and under certain circumstances, be of positive benefit to business organizations. Though not nearly as discussed as the arguments presented above, this argument has made its way into the discussion of psychopathy screening and into the popular media as well. The conclusion of this argument, at least as it has been presented in the public media, is that rather than "destroying" Corporate Psychopaths, business organizations might look to keep them in their employ. This argument is owed almost entirely to Kevin Dutton's *The Wisdom of Psychopaths: What Saints, Spies, and Serial Killers Can Teach Us About Success*, which appeared in 2012. Dutton, a British psychologist, opens *The Wisdom of Psychopaths* by recounting the life of his father, a salesman, whom he comes to realize was a psychopathic personality after his death. That his father navigated his way through life without engaging in the violent or abusive behavior typically associated with psychopathic personalities caused Dutton to reconsider the traditional narrative about "psychopaths," and advance the theory that psychopathic traits, at least in relative moderation, can at times be adaptive, conferring advantages on individuals with them. He recalls a conversation he had with a highly successful young attorney in London in which the attorney readily admitted that, "Deep inside me there's a serial killer lurking somewhere. But I keep him amused with cocaine, Formula One, booty calls, and coruscating cross-examination" (Dutton, 2012, loc. 112). If the "psychopath" knows how to "harness their traits and keep them in check," Dutton theorizes, those traits can be turned to the advantage of their possessor.

Dutton's model of psychopathy is based on what he calls "inner and outer zones" of the disorder (Dutton, 2012, loc. 298). The "inner zone" is where the individuals we typically associate with psychopathy reside (i.e., violent psychopathic personalities). The remainder of us inhabit the "outer zone." Here we find individuals who may display a few of the psychopathic personality traits to a heightened degree while not displaying in noticeable ways the full constellation of psychopathic traits. Dutton's metaphor for describing the dimensionality of psychopathy is that of the dials and sliders on a studio mixing desk: "If you push all of them to the max, you'll have a sound track that's no use to anyone. But if the sound track is graded and some controls are turned up higher than others—such as fearlessness, focus, lack of empathy, and mental toughness, for example—you may well have a surgeon who's a cut above the rest" (Dutton, 2012, loc. 308). Dutton's "wisdom of psychopaths" theory is more than just another account of what it means to be a "functional psychopath," though it does include that. His theory is that the presence of psychopathic personalities in the human population has served an evolutionary purpose over the eons, not only for the personalities themselves but for the rest of us as well. In our long ago evolutionary past, conformity became hardwired into our brains. When threatened, we tended to "huddle up," a survival technique still displayed by herd animals like zebras. Over evolutionary time, the need to behave like herd animals in the face of physical threats from predators diminished as we, as a species, developed more sophisticated and successful modes of collective self-defense. The "neuro-urge" to conform, however, Dutton suggests, has remained, as is borne out by contemporary work in the psychology of groups. But, Dutton argues, not only are there times now when the ability to break free of social convention is a good thing, but the same was the case in our evolutionary past. Modern game theory, he argues, explains why. He draws our attention to the familiar scenario of a game of chicken in which two drivers are hurdling toward one another and each driver has to decide whether to swerve to avoid collision or continue ahead, but with a prisoner's dilemma like distribution of benefits based on how they interact. If both adopt the "non-psychopathic" option and swerve, they each earn three points. If both adopt the "psychopathic" option and continue ahead, they each receive only one point. But, if one adopts the "psychopathic" option and the other adopts the "non-psychopathic" option, the "psychopath" receives four points while the "non-psychopath" receives only two. When the game is played repeatedly by computer programs with encoded, predetermined response strategies, an interesting outcome is generated. As Dutton puts it,

> When the payoffs are converted into units of Darwinian fitness and the assumption is made that those players in receipt of larger payoffs give rise to a

> greater number of offspring who then adopt precisely the same strategy as their progenitors, the population evolves to a stable equilibrium in which the proportion of individuals behaving psychopathically actually mirrors the observed incidence of the disorder in real life (around one to two percent). (Dutton, 2012, loc. 1257-1260)

Dutton also references the work of the psychologist Peter Jonason as added support for this game theory modeling of the reproductive advantage that psychopathic personalities have in certain environmental conditions. In 2009, Jonason and his colleagues published the results of their study of 224 college students (88 men and 136 women) who were asked to report on their sexual relationships, including their attitudes toward casual sex (Jonason et al., 2009). Each participant was measured for levels of narcissism (using the Narcissistic Personality Inventory), psychopathy (using the Self-Report Psychopathy Scale-III), and Machiavellianism (using the MACH-IV). Their study showed that the presence of the Dark Triad was correlated with what the authors label a "short-term mating strategy" which, from the perspective of evolutionary biology, could confer reproductive advantages for males in that they potentially generate more offspring by "accessing" a larger number of mates across a given period of time (the correlation between the Dark Triad and a "short-term mating strategy" was not significant for the female participants).

In the modern world, Dutton focuses on roles, the execution of which may be enhanced for the better by the presence of specific sets of psychopathic traits. For surgeons, laser-focus, lack of empathy, and coldness, some of the traits making up the psychopathic profile, may be advantageous to their craft, and a good thing for their patients as well. For law enforcement, the ability to zero in on the weaknesses of others, an ability psychopathic personalities use to identify and exploit their victims, may prove quite handy in identifying guilty parties. For business leaders, being superficially charming, egocentric, persuasive, and insensitive to the fate of others serves them well as they climb the corporate ladder of success. And, as judged by their biographers, several U.S. presidents had some of their "psychopathic knobs" turned up pretty high.

The benefits of psychopathic traits are conferred not just on those business leaders with some of their "psychopathic knobs" turned to "loud," but also to the companies they work for, Dutton argues. In particular, Dutton cites the work of Osumi and Ohiri, who showed that under certain circumstances, psychopathic personalities make better financial decisions than the rest of us (Osumi & Ohiri, 2010). Osumi and Ohiri ran a version of the "ultimatum game" in which two players interact to decide how to divide a sum of money. The first player proposes a distribution, say "50-50" or "80-20," and the second player can accept or reject the offer. If the second player accepts the offer, then the money is distributed to the two players accordingly. If the second player decides to reject the offer, then neither player receives anything. The results of their study showed that psychopathic personalities, when put in the role of player #2, were more willing to accept offers that would be perceived as unfair by non-psychopathic personalities (e.g., an offer that gave only 20% to player #2). Because they don't experience an emotional reaction to perceived slights, as non-psychopathic personalities do, the psychopathic personalities in the study adopted a straightforward, "rational" approach to the decision to accept or reject. Rejection meant no "income," while acceptance guaranteed some. Translated to the business world, the implication is that psychopathic personalities would, when faced with business proposals or opportunities similar to those in the ultimatum game, make better financial decisions for the firms they work for, not foregoing opportunities for revenue generation just because those opportunities may not appear to be "fair." A psychopathic personality's ability to make such "cold" calculations without concern for the non-financial effects of doing so can be seen as a "talent" that business organizations, especially corporations, might find desirable. Other studies (see Shiv et al., 2005 and Frydman et al., 2011) have supported this finding that individuals who are deficit in emotional processing, including the processing of fear, fare better at games involving "gambling" decisions than individuals displaying neither trait. This is one reason, as Hare, Babiak, Boddy and others have argued, psychopathic personalities find safe haven in the modern world of business.

It should be noted that the examples of "wise," advantageous psychopathic personalities Dutton describes in his book are not, strictly speaking, the kinds of individuals designated as Corporate Psychopaths in the literature on the subject. Recall his imagery for thinking about psychopathic personalities, the image of dials on a studio mixing board, where the "volume" each dial controls can be tuned up or down by degrees. The saints, spies, surgeons, lawyers, and other characters Dutton describes have a small set of the dials on the mixing board turned "up." For saints, the amplification is of the traits of "stoicism, the ability to regulate emotions, to enter altered states of awareness, to be heroic, to be fearless, yes, even empathic" (Dutton, 2012, loc. 3024). For spies, it is the coolness, charisma, and power of persuasion that stick out in the "psychopathy soundtrack." For surgeons, the dials turned up are the ones controlling focus and fearlessness, with the dial for emotional empathy turned down low. The same is true for lawyers with the addition of an amplified sense of grandiosity and a penchant for "cold calculation." As described in chapter one, the dimensionality of psychopathy means that the heightened presence of a few traits belonging to the cluster of personality traits that ground a diagnosis of psychopathy does not equate with such a diagnosis. For this text, we have adopted the convention of reserving the term "psychopathic personality" for those cases where the PCL-R (or related measurement instruments) threshold for a diagnosis of psychopathy has been met. In other contexts, authors like Dutton use the term more loosely, allowing for individuals who dramatically display *some* of the psychopathic traits to qualify for the designation "psychopath" or "psychopathic." In *The Wisdom of Psychopaths*, though he has some occasional reference to screening instruments like the PCL-R, he doesn't consistently establish the purported psychopathy of the characters, real and fictional, he presents as examples of "psychopaths" using professionally recognized diagnostic screens. Though they may have some dials turned up in such a way as to make for a good rock song, they don't have a full orchestra in play. Because of this, the "wisdom" he argues we could glean from the various characters he describes may not actually be "the wisdom of *psychopaths*."

That said, his point about the value that Corporate Psychopaths may bring to the firms they work for is a claim that others involved in the Corporate Psychopath Hypothesis discussion have made as well. Based on some research into how postgraduate business students perceive the personality traits valued by corporations, Boddy reports that the perception is that corporations value traits like the ability to be charming, the determination to be promoted, being opportunistic, exhibiting cunningness when faced with business opportunity, and the absence of guilt or remorse over decisions made. The same research indicated that for most of these traits, the study participants perceived themselves to lack these traits. Boddy concludes that, "If these perceptions of what corporations value in an employee are correct, then Corporate Psychopaths look like desirable employees in terms of being more prepared to be opportunistic and ruthless, to put the organisation before love and to be impersonal and cunning, among other factors" (Boddy, 2011b, p. 141). Clarke acknowledges that "organizational psychopaths," a subgroup of Corporate Psychopaths, may offer firms some short-term value because "[t]hey possess good verbal skills, are experienced at manipulating people, are prepared to do whatever it takes to achieve their goals, and they may be creative as a result of their being prone to boredom leading to the development of new ideas" (Clarke, 2005, p. 169). As we will see in chapter four, Clarke cautions that the business gains "organizational psychopaths" help their firms to realize may be short-lived as the negative consequences of their behavior finally catch up with them in the long-term to the detriment of their employer. In *Snakes in Suits*, Babiak and Hare comment on the changes that "organizational structures and processes" went through in the 1970s and 1980s as large business operations shed their historical commitment to a "bureaucracy model," which required large, costly managerial populations, in favor of sleeker, leaner, more efficient organizational structures and processes in which change is dominant.

> With the need to embrace change came a switch from hiring "organization men and women" who would maintain the status quo to hiring individuals who would shake the trees, rattle the cages, and get things done quickly. This hiring switch inadvertently led to the selection of some individuals with psychopathic traits and characteristics. Unfortunately, the general state of confusion that change brings to any situation can make psychopathic personality traits–the appearance of confidence, strength, and calm–often look like the answer to the organization's problems. Yet, hiring individuals with these traits seemed like the right thing to do. Egocentricity, callousness, and insensitivity suddenly became acceptable trade-offs in order to get the talent and skills needed to survive in an accelerated, dispassionate business world. (Babiak & Hare, 2006, p. xii)

This characterization of the corporate world in the mid-1990s is as accurate as it was then, so it is reasonable to presume that the same corporate "desires" for the "talents" that psychopathic personalities bring with them are still operative. In short, the possibility that a large business organization would perceive it beneficial, even if it involves trade-offs, to have psychopathic personalities on board in the right positions and roles remains a viable hypothesis.

Research published by Bate, Boduszek, Dhingra, and Bale in 2014 showed higher intelligence of psychopathic personalities, as measured by the Raven's progressive Matrices IQ test and the LSRP, and that psychopath personalities are better able to control their emotional responses than those with lower IQ scores (Bate et al., 2014). Sandberg advances the thesis that given the advantages that "successful psychopaths" can bring to their jobs in the board room, the operating room, or the British Parliament, what should be screened for isn't psychopathy by itself, but a combination of high intelligence and the desired psychopathic personality traits:

> What matters morally is more whether the smart psychopath actually has good control over their impulses, and whether their goals align with the organization. Maybe we should focus more on how to test for this than what the core personality is (no matter how fascinating insights we gain from studying psychopaths). After all, knowing that our employee, surgeon or MP is reliably going to use their personality traits and abilities in a way that works for your shared goals, is what we actually want. (Sandberg, 2014)

Sandberg, at least, is correct to recognize that hiring for certain traits that are a part of the cluster of personality traits, even if those particular dials are turned way up, is not the same thing as hiring for psychopathy.

CONCLUSION

In this chapter, the basics of the Corporate Psychopath Hypothesis were laid out. The empirical part of the Corporate Psychopath Hypothesis, that psychopathic personalities inhabit the business world at rates noticeably higher than that for the general population and that they cause a range of harms to fellow employees, to the organizations they work for, and to the larger social/economic systems in which the firms they work for are situated, was discussed. Three anchor studies, one by Babiak and Hare and two by Boddy, form the bulk of the empirical evidence for the claim that psychopathic personalities can be found in the business world at abnormally high rates. The results of these three studies are bolstered by other, mostly smaller studies as well as individual case studies. The same is true for the empirical data that grounds the four arguments in support of employment screening for psychopathy: (1) the presence of Corporate Psychopaths in the workplace is correlated with higher levels of harm and unjust treatment, mostly in the form of bullying and other types of intimidating behavior, (2) the presence of Corporate Psychopaths in the workforce creates significant risks for the organizations that employ them, (3) the presence of Corporate Psychopaths in positions of decision-making power, especially in large financial institutions, have caused damage to the larger social/economic systems in which those institutions conduct business and have the potential to continue to do so, and (4) firms may want to, in certain scenarios, employ Corporate Psychopaths because their personality traits are beneficial to firms' interests. Whether these empirical studies meet the professional requirements of social science research is a question that is left unanswered in this text, though Babiak, Hare, and Boddy argue that they do. Since the purpose of this text is to grant the Corporate Psychopath Hypothesis, and then critically evaluate the legality and ethics of carrying out the call to screen for psychopathic personalities in the workplace, the question of the validity of the empirical research in support of the hypothesis need not be settled for our purposes. The normative grounds for the call to "seek and destroy" Corporate Psychopaths, for example the principle that employers have a moral duty to provide for the occupational safety of their employees, was also laid out. The philosophical force of these normative foundations, of course, is still at times a topic of academic debate. As with the empirical research supporting the Corporate Psychopath Hypothesis, it is not necessary that all philosophical questions about these normative foundations be settled. They are reasonable and well argued for accounts of the source and nature of certain moral duties, and that is sufficient for proceeding with a consideration of the legality and ethics of enacting the call to arms to eliminate Corporate Psychopaths from the workforce. The next two chapters are devoted to that consideration, beginning

Chapter Three

Psychopathy and the Americans with Disabilities Act

In American employment law, employers have a great deal of latitude in how they structure and conduct hiring and firing processes, though that latitude is not unlimited. Federal, state, and local statutes can limit the "what" and the "how" of information gathering employers can engage in during the hiring process (e.g., asking questions about sexual orientation or family status) as well as limiting which criteria they can use in deciding whom to hire or not hire (e.g., race, ethnicity, sex, etc.). Similarly, statutes can limit the reasons employers can rely on for termination decisions (e.g., age) and in some cases require that terminations be conducted in accordance with certain rules (e.g., layoffs exceeding 500 jobs during any 30-day period not due to plant closing requires 60-day notice). In the absence of relevant laws or contractual stipulations, however, employment in the U.S. is characterized by the employment-at-will doctrine. Employers are free to hire and fire "at will," for any reason or no reason whatsoever. Likewise, unless contractually restricted, employees can quit jobs "at will." As a basic principle of distributive justice for the allocation of employment in the U.S., employment-at-will is typically justified on the ground that it creates a balance of power between employers and employees, thereby maximizing the liberty of both parties. Also, a secondary, utilitarian justification for employment-at-will is that by maximizing the liberty of employers and employees, that portion of overall social utility or social happiness linked to employment is maximized as well since employees and employers are able to satisfy their preferences regarding employment as they see fit. Statutes and judicial decisions restricting the exercise of employment-at-will on the part of employers are typically defended on the grounds that they are necessary to maintain the balance of power aimed at by employment-at-will and to protect employees against significant loss of liberty and opportunity due to the decisions employers might otherwise make if such restrictions were not in place.

As discussed in the previous chapter, the call for employment screening for psychopathy is primarily based in an employer's recognized and legitimate interests in reducing the risk of workplace harm and in protecting the organization itself from damage that Corporate Psychopaths can cause. Secondarily, testing for and identifying Corporate Psychopaths is argued for because employers are bound by duties to protect the social good from the types of harms Corporate Psychopaths can cause to the larger social/economic systems within which firms operate. These justifications match the purposes employment-at-will is intended to serve, so it would seem to easily follow that pre-employment and post-hire screening for psychopathy would fall under the "at will" liberties of employers. In general, it is legal for an employer to use personality or psychological tests as part of the pre-employment screening process as long as the use of such tests doesn't have a disparate impact in violation of Title VII of the Civil Rights Act of 1964 because it is used intentionally to target members of groups protected (i.e., the employer believes one or more of the personality traits tested for are identified with members of a protected class and so the employer is using those traits as a proxy for the class itself) under Title VII or the tests are used to identify personality traits not reasonably tied to the performance of the job. Courts have held that an applicant's personality is not a trait protected under Title VII. Further, psychopathy is not a protected trait or characteristic listed under Title VII so it would be very difficult to successfully press the case that the use of the PCL-R or any similar test as part of employment screening would violate Title VII. However, when considering the Americans with Disabilities Act, including changes made by the ADA Amendments Act of 2008, a different story emerges. This chapter is devoted to a consideration of the extent to which psychopathy can be construed as a "disability" under the ADA, and, hence, the claim that to engage in pre-employment screening of job applicants and post-hire testing of employees for psychopathy would be illegal.

THE AMERICANS WITH DISABILITIES ACT: THE BASICS

Enacted in 1990, the stated purpose behind the ADA is,

1. to provide a clear and comprehensive national mandate for the elimination of discrimination against individuals with disabilities;
2. to provide clear, strong, consistent, enforceable standards addressing discrimination against individuals with disabilities;

3. to ensure that the Federal Government plays a central role in enforcing the standards established in this chapter on behalf of individuals with disabilities; and
4. to invoke the sweep of congressional authority, including the power to enforce the fourteenth amendment and to regulate commerce, in order to address the major areas of discrimination faced day-to-day by people with disabilities (ADA, 1990, sec. 12101).

Generally speaking, "[T]he ADA broadly protects the rights of individuals with disabilities in employment, access to State and local government services, places of public accommodation, transportation, and other important areas of American life. The ADA also requires newly designed and constructed or altered State and local government facilities, public accommodations, and commercial facilities to be readily accessible to and usable by individuals with disabilities" (ADA Title II Regulations).

Regarding employment, the ADA makes illegal discrimination "against a qualified individual on the basis of disability in regard to job application procedures, the hiring, advancement, or discharge of employees, employee compensation, job training, and other terms, conditions, and privileges of employment" (ADA, sec. 12112, (a) "general rule"). More specifically, employers are prohibited from,

1. limiting, segregating, or classifying a job applicant or employee in a way that adversely affects the opportunities or status of such applicant or employee because of the disability of such applicant or employee;
2. participating in a contractual or other arrangement or relationship that has the effect of subjecting a covered entity's qualified applicant or employee with a disability to the discrimination prohibited by this subchapter (such relationship includes a relationship with an employment or referral agency, labor union, an organization providing fringe benefits to an employee of the covered entity, or an organization providing training and apprenticeship programs);
3. utilizing standards, criteria, or methods of administration
   a. that have the effect of discrimination on the basis of disability;
   b. that perpetuates the discrimination of others who are subject to common administrative control;
4. excluding or otherwise denying equal jobs or benefits to a qualified individual because of the known disability of an individual with whom the qualified individual is known to have a relationship or association;
   a. not making reasonable accommodations to the known physical or mental limitations of an otherwise qualified individual with a disability

who is an applicant or employee, unless such covered entity can demonstrate that the accommodation would impose an undue hardship on the operation of the business of such covered entity; or

b. denying employment opportunities to a job applicant or employee who is an otherwise qualified individual with a disability, if such denial is based on the need of such covered entity to make reasonable accommodation to the physical or mental impairments of the employee or applicant;

5. using qualification standards, employment tests or other selection criteria that screen out or tend to screen out an individual with a disability or a class of individuals with disabilities unless the standard, test or other selection criteria, as used by the covered entity, is shown to be job-related for the position in question and is consistent with business necessity; and
6. failing to select and administer tests concerning employment in the most effective manner to ensure that, when such test is administered to a job applicant or employee who has a disability that impairs sensory, manual, or speaking skills, such test results accurately reflect the skills, aptitude, or whatever other factor of such applicant or employee that such test purports to measure, rather than reflecting the impaired sensory, manual, or speaking skills of such employee or applicant (except where such skills are the factors that the test purports to measure) (ADA, sec. 12112, (b) "construction").

For present purposes, of importance is subsection (6), the qualified prohibition of the use of standards, tests, or other selection criteria that "screen out or tend to screen out an individual with a disability or a class of individuals with disabilities." "Standards, tests, or other selection criteria" is understood to include but is not limited to:

- education and work experience requirements;
- physical and mental requirements;
- safety requirements;
- paper and pencil tests;
- physical or psychological tests;
- interview questions; and
- rating systems.

If it could be shown that psychopathy qualifies as a "disability" under the ADA, and that the type of pre-employment or post-hire screening called for as part of the "seeking out" of Corporate Psychopaths described in the previous chapter does not count as "job-related for the position in question and is consistent with business necessity," then such screening would run afoul of the ADA. Because it targets both physical and *mental* disabilities, the ADA may well present a barrier to an employer's interest, as *prima facie* legitimate as it might be, in screening for psychopathy if psychopathy can be understood to qualify as a "mental disability." Further, since the ADA is intended to not only prevent pre-employment testing of certain kinds but to also, and it may be said more importantly, create a legal basis for providing workplace accommodations for covered disabilities, if psychopathy can be understood to fall into the category of "mental disability" then not only would employers face restrictions regarding testing for it, they would also be responsible for providing reasonable accommodations for employees who have the mental disability of psychopathy.

PSYCHOPATHY AS DISABILITY UNDER THE ADA

The ADA, including the changes made by the ADA Amendments Act of 2008, uses the language of "disability," not the language of "disorder" or "disposition," which are the terms typically used in defining psychopathy. The ADA National Network, an organization that provides information, guidance, and training on the ADA, notes that the term "psychiatric disability" is typically used in a legal or policy context to refer to impairments covered by the ADA. In the literature on psychopathy, a full-blown psychopathic personality is not referred to as a disability by psychologists. This leaves us to determine if psychopathy would qualify under the ADA's definition of "disability" even though it is not directly referred to as such by psychologists who study it. As discussed in chapter one, there is ongoing debate as to whether psychopathy is a mental *disorder* or *illness*. For the camp opposed to such designations, psychopathy is simply a mental *difference* that some individuals may exhibit. As noted in that chapter, it is not necessary, in a strict sense, for that debate to be settled in order for the argument to be developed in this chapter and those to be developed in the next chapter to have bite. What is necessary for the argument to be advanced in this chapter is that it makes sense to think of psychopathy as an *impairment*. Psychological conditions that are not disorders, strictly understood, can still be considered to be impairments, as will be made clear in the following analysis of the ADA treatment of "mental impairment."

By "disabled," the ADA means "a person who has a physical or mental impairment that substantially limits one or more major life activities, a person who has a history or record of such an impairment, or a person who is perceived by others as having such an impairment." This definition of "disability" has three key terms or ideas that need clarifying. First, a physical or mental *impairment* must be present. Second, the presence of that impairment must *substantially limit* one or more major life activities. And third, it must be a *major life activity* that is impaired. The amended ADA intends these terms to be "construed in favor of broad coverage of individuals," primarily as a reaction to narrow interpretations located in court cases prior to 2008.

For "major life activity," paragraph (2) of the amended ADA states the following:

Major Life Activities

(A) In general
For purposes of paragraph (1), major life activities include, but are not limited to, caring for oneself, performing manual tasks, seeing, hearing, eating, sleeping, walking, standing, lifting, bending, speaking, breathing, learning, reading, concentrating, thinking, communicating, and working.

(B) Major bodily functions
For purposes of paragraph (1), a major life activity also includes the operation of a major bodily function, including but not limited to, functions of the immune system, normal cell growth, digestive, bowel, bladder, neurological, brain, respiratory, circulatory, endocrine, and reproductive functions.

The EEOC Enforcement Guidance on the Americans with Disabilities Act and Psychiatric Disabilities (EEOC Notice number 915.002, issued in 1997) notes that there is no exhaustive list of major live activities that could be judged to be impaired by a psychiatric disability, but examples include "learning, thinking, concentrating, interacting with others, caring for oneself, speaking, performing manual task or working."

As for "substantially limits," paragraph (4) of the amended ADA states that "shall be interpreted consistently with the findings and purposes of the ADA Amendments Act of 2008," and that,

The determination of whether an impairment substantially limits a major life activity shall be made without regard to the ameliorative effects of mitigating measures such as

I. medication, medical supplies, equipment, or appliances, low-vision devices (which do not include ordinary eyeglasses or contact lenses), prosthetics including limbs and devices, hearing aids and cochlear implants or other implantable hearing devices, mobility devices, or oxygen therapy equipment and supplies;

II. use of assistive technology;
III. reasonable accommodations or auxiliary aids or services; or
IV. learned behavioral or adaptive neurological modifications.

The ameliorative effects of the mitigating measures of ordinary eyeglasses or contact lenses shall be considered in determining whether an impairment substantially limits a major life activity.

The EEOC Enforcement Guidance notice describes "substantially limiting" as "prevent[ing] an individual from performing a major life activity or significantly restricts the condition, manner, or duration under which an individual can perform a major life activity, as compared to the average person in the general population."

"Mental impairment" includes any mental or psychological disorder, such as intellectual disability (formerly termed mental retardation), organic brain syndrome, emotional or mental illness, and specific learning disabilities. The EEOC Enforcement Guidance document indicates that for enforcement purposes, "mental impairment" is to be understood as including any mental or psychological *disorder*, including emotional and mental *illnesses*. Examples include major depression, bipolar disorder, anxiety disorders (which include panic disorder, obsessive compulsive disorder, and post-traumatic stress disorder), schizophrenia, and *personality disorders*. The ADA was amended in 2008 to include Attention-Deficit/Hyperactivity Disorder (ADHD) as an example of a physical or mental impairment that qualifies as a disability. The guidance document notes that the *DSM* is relied upon by courts in identifying these disorders. As described in chapter one, crafters of the DSM, since its inception, have held out against listing psychopathy as an official clinical diagnosis, though the DSM does list psychopathy as a specifier of antisocial personality disorder. If, for enforcement purposes, "mental impairment" is understood to include the category of "personality disorders," then antisocial personality disorder would qualify as a "mental impairment" under the ADA. As a "specifier" of ASPD, courts could, broadly, judge that psychopathy qualifies as well. This would only be the first step in judging whether psychopathy would be a protected disability under the ADA since the simple presence of a physical or mental impairment does not rise to the level of an ADA-covered "disability" unless it also meets the test of substantially limiting a major life activity.

Would the possession of a psychopathic "disorder" or "disposition" qualify one for protection under the ADA's definition of "disability?" To answer that question, it would have to be determined that an individual with a psychopathic personality suffers from a physical or mental impairment that substantially limits their pursuit of a major life activity, as described above. As a dimensional psychological construct (i.e., psychopathic traits are distributed along a continuum from low to high) and not a categorical one (i.e., an individual either has psychopathic traits or they do not), psychopathic traits may be expected to be "mildly" present in large numbers of any given population (Guay et al., 2007; Edens et al., 2006). At low levels, the presence of traits like reduced empathy, a less than robust moral conscience, and an inconsistent experience of guilt and remorse would likely not count as "impairments," at least not in the sense intended in the ADA. To treat them as such would qualify all but the mostly saintly of us for ADA protection. But, as one moves along the continuum, and the degree to which psychopathic traits are present intensifies, the greater the chance that the presence of these more intensely experienced and displayed traits rise to the level of a "disability" as defined by the ADA and the EEOC guidelines. The cluster of traits associated with a psychopathic disposition are ones that, if present in more than "low" levels, quite reasonably could impair someone's ability to, for example, interact with others, an activity that qualifies as a "major life activity" in the understanding of the ADA used by the EEOC. What this means is that even individuals whose PCL-R score is not at or above the threshold used for diagnoses of psychopathy may still qualify for ADA protection.

ADA coverage distinguishes between *physical* and *mental* impairments. To qualify for protection and accommodations under the ADA, and individual need not have both types of impairments. The presence of either suffices. Consequently, in the case of psychopathy, it can be considered just as a mental impairment in the context of such protection and accommodations. There need not be an accompanying physical, in this case neurological, impairment present to qualify. That said, if it were the case that psychopathy, as a psychological condition, is caused by or co-occurs with one or more neurological impairments, then the case for including psychopathy as an ADA-covered impairment is strengthened. Though far from a settled question, there is an emerging understanding of the neurological basis of psychopathy. Neuroimaging in the early 2000s confirmed hypotheses that there existed a neurological basis for psychopathy by showing that psychopathy was linked to dysfunction in the amygdala, an area of the brain involved in aversive conditioning and instrumental learning as well as response to facial expressions of emotion like fear and sadness. These early studies showed that psychopathy was associated with reduced amygdala volume (Tiihonen et al., 2000; Kiehl et al., 2001). More recent imaging research has extended this early finding to show that there are other neurological conditions underlying psychopathy. In 2013, a study of 121 inmates of a medium-security prison in the US used functional magnetic resonance imaging to map neural responses of highly, moderately, and weakly psychopathic inmates (assessed using the PCL-R) when asked to first imagine themselves in pain and then imagine pain in others (Decety et al., 2013). As expected, when imagining pain to themselves, highly psychopathic inmates showed the usual neural response in brain areas associated with the experience of empathy. However, when asked to imagine pain to others, these areas failed to become active. Additionally, they showed an increase in neural activity in an area of the brain, the ventral striatum, known to be associated with the experience of pleasure. Research published in 2015 by Gregory et al. established that a group of clinically diagnosed psychopathic individuals who were part of Britain's National Probation Service formerly incarcerated for crimes such as murder and rape displayed significantly less amounts of grey matter in their anterior rostral prefrontal cortex and temporal poles than that found in offenders with non-psychotic, antisocial disorder and that found in healthy non-criminals (Gregory et al., 2015).

This evidence indicates that psychopathic individuals suffer from a physical disorder, as well as a mental one. The same considerations covered above concerning the extent to which the psychiatric disorder of psychopathy would qualify as a psychiatric *disability* under the ADA and EEOC guidelines apply as well when considering whether the physical (neurological) disorder of psychopathy would qualify as a physical disability under the ADA. That the operation of a major bodily function, including neurological and brain functions, counts as a "major life activity" under the ADA would indicate that individuals suffering from the neurological conditions associated with psychopathy described above, whether they have ever engaged in psychopathic behavior, would fall under the ADA categorization of "disabled."

Generally speaking, we are interested in whether individuals who entirely lack a sense of empathy, act as if they have no moral conscience, and experience no regret or guilt for their actions have an impairment that substantially limits their pursuit of one or more major life activities. Considered abstractly, as argued above, the answer would be yes. As social beings, the ability to form meaningful relationships with others is central to our nature and highly constitutive of human happiness. Ironically, because they possess strong interpersonal skills such as charm and glibness, psychopathic persons can be quite skilled at *appearing* to be involved in relationships in ways that mimic authentic, meaningful commitment. These relationships, however, are never seen by the psychopathic personality as anything more than superficial, exploitative, and entirely self-serving. By definition, psychopathic personalities are *unable* to engage in the major life activity of interacting with others in a manner that manifests and is grounded in a genuine interest in the other, not just *substantially limited* in their ability to do so. In this way, individuals possessed of psychopathy would seem to be protected against pre-employment screening, post-hire testing, and other forms of workplace discrimination, such as termination linked to their psychological disorder, under the ADA.

THE USE OF MEDICAL EXAMINATIONS TO TEST FOR PSYCHOPATHY

As noted at the outset of this chapter, employers have a good deal of latitude in establishing hiring procedures. Generally, as long as an employer can establish that an application requirement (e.g. submitting to a personality test or a credit check), is a reasonable job requirement linked to a legitimate business necessity, and the requirement does not serve to discriminate against individuals or create disparate impact on groups of individuals as described in Title VII of the Civil Rights Act and the ADA, including all subsequent EEOC rulings and guidelines, then the employer is free to make such a requirement of job applicants. The EEOC defines "personality test" as a test intended to "assess the degree to which a person has certain traits or dispositions (e.g., dependability, cooperativeness, safety) or aim to predict the likelihood that a person will engage in certain conduct (e.g., theft, absenteeism)" (EEOC, 2007). Also, as noted earlier, "personality" has not been held to be a protected characteristic, so employers can make use of instruments to "probe" a job applicant's personality in order to ascertain if they possess the desired personality traits and do not possess those an employer deems undesirable for the job in question.

Historically, however, the use of personality tests in the employment setting has faced some challenges. As recently as 2015, Cavico, Mujtaba, Lawrence, and Muffler have described the use of personality testing in the employment area as a "continuing legal, ethical, and practical quandary" (Cavico et al., 2015). One ongoing concern regards the practical efficacy of such tests. In their 1990 survey, Hough et al. report that, primarily due to the pervasiveness of respondent "faking," there was insufficient evidence to conclude that self-reporting personality tests provided reliable information upon which to base employment decisions (Hough et al., 1990). They also note that efforts to reduce the frequency of respondent "faking" by the development of test formats involving a forced-choice structure (i.e., a format in which the items respondents select between are of similar social desirability) and instruments involving subtle items (i.e., items for which the underlying construct, such as "risk-taking enjoyment" or "positive view of criminality" are not readily apparent to the test taker) did little to improve the reliability and validity of the current stock of personality tests in use. The situation improved by the late 1990s, according to Goodstein and Lanyon, with the development and adoption of the "Five-Factor" approach, a model of personality research that focuses on five core traits: openness, conscientiousness, extraversion, agreeableness, and neuroticism (Goodstein & Lanyon, 1999). Reviews of research on the "Big Five," they note, showed that the personality abstractions used in the "Five-Factor" approach "represented consistencies in the ways that people experience their world and act," revealed that "the stronger the trait in a person, the more likely that person is to show trait-related behaviors," and supported the claim that the five traits are "consistent and relatively independent traits" (Goodstein & Lanyon, 1999, p. 294).

Apart from the concerns for reliability and validity, the use of personality tests in the employment setting continues to face criticisms that their use is neither fair nor legal. As there is little published case law on the matter of ADA prohibition of the use of personality tests in the employment setting (Willner et al., 2016), two judicial decisions do stand out as setting legal constraint on the use of such tests as pertains to ADA-based disability protection. In *Karraker v. Rent-A-Center, Inc.*, from 2005, the U.S. Court of Appeals, Seventh Circuit, ruled that the use of the MMPI by the defendant as part of its promotion process constituted illegal discrimination due to the fact that elevated scores on certain scales of the MMPI can be interpreted as signs of psychiatric disorders. In effect, the MMPI was used in this setting as a medical examination. The Court relied on two EEOC examples of uses of psychological tests that make them medical examinations:

Example 1: A psychological test is designed to reveal mental illness, but a particular employer says it does not give the test to disclose mental illness (for example, the employer says it uses the test to disclose just tastes and habits). But, the test also is interpreted by a psychologist, and is routinely used in a clinical setting to provide evidence that would lead to a diagnosis of a mental disorder or impairment (for example, whether an applicant has paranoid tendencies, or is depressed). Under these facts, this test is a medical examination.

Example 2: An employer gives applicants the RUOK Test (hypothetical), an examination that reflects whether applicants have characteristics that lead to identifying whether the individual has excessive anxiety, depression, and certain compulsive disorders (DSM-listed conditions). This test is medical.

In the Court's judgment, Rent-A-Center's use of the MMPI resembled the first example (even though no psychologist was brought in to interpret the test results), and because of that "likely had the effect of excluding employees with disorders from promotions." The Court concluded that

> [b]ecause it is designed, at least in part, to reveal mental illness and has the effect of hurting the employment prospects of one with a mental disability, we think the MMPI is best categorized as a medical examination. And even though the MMPI was only a part (albeit a significant part) of a battery of tests administered to employees looking to advance, its use, we conclude, violated the ADA. (Karraker, 2005)

The *Karraker* ruling identifies two conditions used to judge the MMPI to be a medical examination: (1) the MMPI can be used to identify the presence of a mental illness and (2) the use of the MMPI has the effect of hurting the employment prospects of applicants or promotion candidates with mental disabilities. In its concluding statement, the Court moves between "mental illness" and "mental disability." It is unclear whether the judges believed, in general, the two to be synonymous, or that some mental illnesses can be considered mental disabilities, and vice versa. It is clear that the judges reasoned that the identification of mental illnesses via the use of a personality test like the MMPI qualifies such tests as *medical* examinations since they are, "at least in part," intended to identify the presence of an illness, and that the result of such an examination could also identify someone with an ADA-covered mental *disability*.

Willner, Sonrienberg, Wemmer, and Kochuba criticize the *Karraker* decision.

> [In *Karraker*] the court struggled with the appropriate standard to use, and ultimately conflated the ADA antidiscrimination provision with the ADA pre-offer medical examination disability inquiry prohibition. The result of that case is a rule based on the effect, or disparate impact, of the personality test on disabled applicants, rather than on whether the test actually seeks disability information as provided in the law. The *Karraker* test not only finds no support in the statutory language but also usurps the ADA anti-discrimination provision's role of banning adverse impact discrimination and does so without importing the anti-discrimination provision's business necessity defense. (Willner et al., 2016, p. 5).

They note that in *Thompson v. Borg-Warner Protective Services Corporation*, a district court ruling, the distinction between the ADA's anti-discrimination provision and its ban of pre-offer medical examinations is maintained and that the court in that decision correctly determined that "only personality tests that are designed or used to elicit information about a mental impairment, as opposed to merely revealing personality characteristics that may be disfavored for employment, are medical examinations" (Willner et al., 2016, p. 5). The key, they highlight, is that the design and intent of the test must be to detect a mental impairment, not just that the test might have that effect.

One would expect that the *Karraker* and *Thompson* rulings could be extended to potential cases involving mental disorders like psychopathy. If personality tests that are designed and intended to identify individuals with mental illnesses or disorders would fall under the purview of the ADA, then psychological screens for psychopathy like the PCL-R would certainly also fall under the purview of the ADA. This is not surprising since psychopathy screens like the PCL-R are intended to be *medical* examinations in the first place. A closer look at the ADA prohibition of pre-offer medical examinations and the requirements it puts in place for the administration of medical examinations post-offer will help to see with more clarity why the use of psychopathy screens would be ADA prohibited in the pre-offer setting, and greatly restricted post-offer.

If an employer would desire to engage in pre-employment screening or post-hire testing for psychopathy, they would do so by requiring a medical examination (i.e., the PCL-R, the PCL:SV, or some other diagnostic exam like Boddy's PM-MRV or the B-Scan) or by making inquiries into an applicant's history of mental health. In addition to its general, conditioned prohibition against using "qualification standards, employment tests or other selection criteria that screen out or tend to screen out an individual with a disability or a class of individuals with disabilities," the ADA specifically addresses the administration of medical examinations and inquiries during the hiring process and to current employees (sec. 12112, subsec. [d]).

1. In general. The prohibition against discrimination as referred to in subsection (a) of this section shall include medical examinations and inquiries.
2. Preemployment
   (A) Prohibited examination or inquiry. Except as provided in paragraph (3), a covered entity shall not conduct a medical examination or make inquiries of a job applicant as to whether such applicant is an individual with a disability or as to the nature or severity of such disability.
   (B) Acceptable inquiry. A covered entity may make preemployment inquiries into the ability of an applicant to perform job-related functions.
3. Employment entrance examination. A covered entity may require a medical examination after an offer of employment has been made to a job applicant and prior to the commencement of the employment duties of

such applicant, and may condition an offer of employment on the results of such examination, if

(A) all entering employees are subjected to such an examination regardless of disability;

(B) information obtained regarding the medical condition or history of the applicant is collected and maintained on separate forms and in separate medical files and is treated as a confidential medical record, except that

  (i) supervisors and managers may be informed regarding necessary restrictions on the work or duties of the employee and necessary accommodations;

  (ii) first aid and safety personnel may be informed, when appropriate, if the disability might require emergency treatment; and

  (iii) government officials investigating compliance with this chapter shall be provided relevant information on request; and

(C) the results of such examination are used only in accordance with this subchapter.

4. Examination and inquiry

   (A) Prohibited examinations and inquiries. A covered entity shall not require a medical examination and shall not make inquiries of an employee as to whether such employee is an individual with a disability or as to the nature or severity of the disability, unless such examination or inquiry is shown to be job-related and consistent with business necessity.

The Technical Assistance Manual for Title I of the ADA, issued in 1992, provides clarification for employers regarding ADA-acceptable uses of medical examinations and medical inquiries during the hiring process.

1. Before making a job offer, an employer may not make any medical inquiry or conduct any medical examination.
2. After making a conditional job offer, before a person starts work, an employer may make unrestricted medical inquiries, but may not refuse to hire an individual with a disability based on results of such inquiries, unless the reason for rejection is job-related and justified by business necessity.
3. After employment, any medical examination or inquiry required of an employee must be job-related and justified by business necessity. Exceptions are voluntary examinations conducted as part of employee health programs and examinations required by other federal laws (Technical Assistance Manual, subsection 6.2, "Basic Requirements").

Further, the Technical Assistance Manual notes that in order to be legal, post-offer medical examinations or medical inquiries need not be a requirement for *all* employees entering the organization, only for all employees entering the organization in the *same job category*. Though the ADA does not require that the employer have a justification for requiring a post-offer medical examination or making post-offer medical inquiries, if a job offer is rescinded due to the results of a medical examination or medical inquiry, it must be the case that the employer can establish that the physical or mental disability precludes the applicant from being able to satisfactorily meet the job qualifications or that due to the disability present the applicant would not be able to perform the job without posing a "direct threat" to the health or safety of self and others. In both cases, it must also be shown that there is no reasonable accommodation available that, if put in place, would allow the applicant to perform the necessary job functions without posing a risk to the safety of self and others in the workplace, unless the provision of such accommodation would cause an "undue hardship" to the employer.

When an individual is rejected as a "direct threat" to health and safety:

1. the employer must be prepared to show a significant current risk of substantial harm (not a speculative or remote risk);
2. the specific risk must be identified;
3. the risk must be documented by objective medical or other factual evidence regarding the particular individual;
4. even if a genuine significant risk of substantial harm exists, the employer must consider whether it can be eliminated or reduced below the level of a "direct threat" by reasonable accommodation (Technical Assistance Manual, subsection 6.2,"Basic Requirements").

The requirements for rescinding an offer based on ability to perform job functions are similar. Rescinding an offer post medical examination or inquiry must be based on "specific medical documentation, reflecting current medical knowledge" that the applicant is not currently able to perform the job functions. It cannot be based on unsubstantiated speculation that the applicant would not be able to perform the job in the future. The Technical Assistance Manual provides some examples as illustration.

- An individual who has an abnormal back X-ray may not be disqualified from a job that requires heavy lifting because of fear that she will be more likely to injure her back or cause higher workers' compensation or health insurance costs. However, where there is documentation that this individual has injured and re-injured her back in similar jobs, and the back condition has been aggravated further by injury, and if there is no reasonable accommodation that would eliminate the risk of reinjury or reduce it to an acceptable level, an employer would be justified in rejecting her for this position.

- If a medical examination reveals that an individual has epilepsy and is seizure-free or has adequate warning of a seizure, it would be unlawful to disqualify this person from a job operating a machine because of fear or speculation that he might pose a risk to himself or others. But if the examination and other medical inquiries reveal that an individual with epilepsy has seizures resulting in loss of consciousness, there could be evidence of significant risk in employing this person as a machine operator. However, even where the person might endanger himself by operating a machine, an accommodation, such as placing a shield over the machine to protect him, should be considered (Technical Assistance Manual, subsection 6.4, "Post-Offer Examinations and Inquiries Permitted").

Regarding the use of medical examinations or the making of medical inquiries to make hiring or termination decisions, we see the same "job-related and consistent with business necessity" qualification that is found in the general prohibition against using potentially discriminatory tests of any type as part of the pre-employment screening process. An employer is allowed to base a decision to rescind a job offer or terminate an employee as a result of the findings of a medical examination or medical inquiry if it can be shown that the decision is job-related to the position in question or stems from a business necessity. In this way, no special exemption is made for medical examinations or medical inquiries. How is that qualification to be understood? What qualifies as "job-related and consistent with business necessity," and what does not? The Technical Assistance Manual provides the following explication of "job-related":

> If a qualification standard, test or other selection criterion operates to screen out an individual with a disability, or a class of such individuals on the basis of disability, it must be a legitimate measure or qualification for the specific job it is being used for. It is not enough that it measures qualifications for a general class of jobs.
>
> The ADA does not require that a qualification standard or selection criterion apply only to the "essential functions" of a job. A "job-related" standard or selection criterion may evaluate or measure all functions of a job and employers may continue to select and hire people who can perform all of these functions. It is only when an individual's disability prevents or impedes performance of marginal job functions that the ADA requires the employer to evaluate this individual's qualifications solely on his/her ability to perform the essential functions

> of the job, with or without an accommodation (Technical Assistance Manual, subsection 4.3, "Job-Related").

Within the purview of the ADA, as it is for the Rehabilitation Act of 1973 and Title VII of the Civil Rights Act, "business necessity" is to be understood as pertaining to the essential functions of a job. A standard may be "job-related" but not qualify as a "business necessity" because it does not concern the essential functions of a job. For example,

> An employer may ask candidates for a clerical job if they have a driver's license, because it would be desirable to have a person in the job who could occasionally run errands or take packages to the post office in an emergency. This requirement is "job-related," but it relates to an incidental, not an essential, job function. If it disqualifies a person who could not obtain a driver's license because of a disability, it would not be justified as a "business necessity" for purposes of the ADA (Technical Assistance Manual, subsection 4.3, "Business Necessity").

Allowing that psychopathy qualifies as an ADA-covered disability, if the research that Hare, Babiak, Boddy, and others have conducted bears out the claim that psychopathic personalities in the workplace are real threats to coworkers and a danger to organizational health, then it would seem that employers could rely on the "job-related and consistent with business necessity" defense to justify their intent to use a diagnosis of psychopathy as the reason for rescinding a job offer or for terminating an employee. Recall that a "job-related" standard or selection criterion is not restricted in its use to just the essential functions of a job. Such standards and selection criteria can be used to measure an applicant's ability to perform *all* functions of a job or to measure an employee's continued ability to do the same. It is a broader justification than an appeal to "business necessity," which does require that the standard or selection criterion used be tied to the essential functions of a job. It is quite reasonable to expect that a function of any job is the ability to work well with coworkers and to treat them respectfully in the workplace. It is a well-confirmed fact that, in general, the stronger the social connections an employee has at work, the better their job performance will be (Kohll, 2018; Sepälä & Cameron, 2015). If it stands to reason that the behavior of coworkers impacts an employee's ability to establish social connections in the workplace, then the presence of psychopathic personalities in the workplace will mean not only that *they* will not form strong social connections, something they are incapable of doing in the first place, but they will also inhibit the ability of coworkers to do so as they go about manipulating their work environment to serve their own selfish interests.

Boddy has described the ways in which Corporate Psychopaths use sarcasm, rudeness, and humiliation to belittle others in the workplace (see chapter two) in an attempt to intimidate coworkers, making them more submissive to the desires of the Corporate Psychopath. He has also conducted research showing that employee affective well-being is lower in a work environment where Corporate Psychopaths are present (Boddy, 2014). Creating emotional turmoil in the workplace allows the Corporate Psychopath to take advantage of the social anxiety it engenders among coworkers, playing off coworkers they find useful against those they perceive to be of little value in advancing their own agenda. All of this creates a workplace environment where it is much more difficult to establish strong social connections. Additionally, as Boddy notes, research shows that being treated rudely in the workplace reduces one's job performance and leads to a decrease in interpersonal helpfulness, something that it is easy to imagine would inhibit the formation of strong social connections among coworkers. Relatedly, Boddy reported on research that linked the presence of Corporate Psychopaths in the workplace, especially in supervisory roles, to lower levels of job satisfaction among employees. Sadly, he also draws our attention to research indicating that the aggressive, disruptive behavior of Corporate Psychopaths may be mimicked by their subordinates and other employees because it is seen as a behavioral model for success within the organization. As this behavior spreads through an organization, an environment is created in which, rather than thinking of themselves as members of a "community" engaged in a collective enterprise, employees think of themselves as individuals engaged in competition with one another for organizational advancement. Given the findings of Boddy's research and the research of others, it is quite reasonable to conclude that employers could invoke the "job-related and consistent with business necessity" defense in justifying rescinding a job offer or in justifying the firing of an employee.

Without question, psychopathic personalities in the workplace have the potential to be a "direct threat" to the health and safety of others. As described above, if an employer desires to make use of this defense in rescinding a job offer or terminating an employee they must establish more than just the potential for harm posed by the applicant or employee. They must establish, based on objective medical or other factual evidence, that there exists a "significant current risk of substantial harm." Speculative or remote risk is insufficient. In the case of job applicants and employees with psychopathic personalities, it would have to be established in individual cases that such a "significant current risk" exists. An employer cannot base their decision on a generalized risk that psychopathic personalities as a category pose. Psychopathy is a risk factor, but not a guarantee that an individual suffering from it will act violently or threaten others. If the PCL-R is the diagnostic test of choice, it would need to have a high rate of predictive validity in order to be used to establish a "significant current risk" posed by a particular job applicant or employee. Recently, some research has emerged that casts doubt on the predictive validity of the PCL-R (Jeandarme et al., 2017; Neal et al., 2015.; and Hawes, Boccaccini et al., 2013). This research indicates, among other things, that low validity ratings can be partly attributed to differences in evaluational contexts and interrater disagreement. Since both factors would be present in anything like a common use of the PCL-R or its business adapted derivative, the B-Scan, in the business setting (i.e., it would be used in different types of business settings and different examiners would be involved in administering the exam), there is reason to concede that the PCL-R or any of its adapted versions, as they are currently constructed and applied, when used as a medical examination of job applicants and employees, may not be able to reliably establish the existence of a "substantial current risk" because they may not reliably identify the presence of psychopathy. If so, then their use would not meet the requirements for establishing that a job applicant or employee poses a "direct threat" since PCL-R results would not constitute "objective medical facts." Consequently, an employer would not be able to justify rescinding a job offer or terminating an employee on the grounds they pose a "direct threat" as indicated by PCL-R results.

ADA ACCOMMODATIONS AND PSYCHOPATHIC PERSONALITIES IN THE WORKPLACE

The ADA is only partly concerned with employment testing for physical and mental impairments. It is also, and some may argue more so, concerned with workplace accommodations for those with physical and mental disabilities. The ADA obligates an employer to provide a reasonable accommodation to the known physical or mental limitations of a qualified applicant or employee with a disability unless it can be shown that the accommodation would impose an undue hardship on the business. The Technical Assistance Manual notes that a "reasonable accommodation is any modification or adjustment to a job, an employment practice, or the work environment that makes it possible for an individual with a disability to enjoy an equal employment opportunity" (Technical Assistance Manual, sec. 3.1). Though the accommodation function of the ADA is not the primary focus of this text, it is worth examining briefly the extent to which psychopathic personalities in the workplace would be covered by the ADA, and because of that are due reasonable accommodations to allow them to perform their job functions. If there are reasonable accommodations that would allow an employee diagnosed as psychopathic to adequately perform their job functions and not pose a direct threat to their own health or that of others in the workplace, and these accommodations could be provided without creating an undue hardship for employers, then employers would be obligated to provide for them.

To this day, relatively few studies have been conducted to measure the effects of various psychotherapies on psychopathy, a state of affairs that Hare called "appalling" over two decades ago (Hare, 1999, p. 202). Skeem, Monahan, and Mulvey made a similar observation three years later when they remarked that, "[u]nfortunately, very little PCL-based treatment research has been conducted with noncorrectional populations" (Skeem et al., 2002, p. 582). By very little, they mean one. The treatment research that has been conducted since the early 1990s is restricted to assessing the efficacy of treatment of psychopathic offenders. An oft cited, early study from 1992 by Rice, Harris, and Cormier involving a retrospective evaluation of the efficacy of a maximum security therapeutic community program in reducing recidivism among mentally disordered offenders, some of whom were psychopaths, showed that though treatment was associated with a lower rate of recidivism for non-psychopathic inmates, it was associated with a *higher* rate of violent recidivism for psychopathic inmates (Rice et al., 1992). A 2000 study by Hare, Clark, Gann, and Thornton reported on the effects of "short-term anger management and social skills training programs" on 728 male offenders involved in seven English prisons (Hare et al., 2000, p. 637). Their study showed that such treatment correlated with *higher* rates of recidivism for psychopathic inmates who scored high on Factor One from the PCL-R. In 2006, based on a survey of the available empirical evidence, Harris and Rice conclude that "there is no evidence that any treatments yet applied to psychopaths have been shown to be effective in reducing violence or crime" (Harris & Rice, 2006, p. 568). That remains the consensus view to this day.

A big hurdle to further study of the effect of therapies on individuals with psychopathic personalities is that they are strongly disinclined to participate in such therapies, even when forced to be present, because they do not believe there is anything wrong with them psychologically that needs "fixing" (in fact, they believe they are superior to others in matters psychological, including therapists). Medications don't exist to address the neurological bases of psychopathy, and probably never will, since the emotional traits of psychopathic personalities such as lack of caring, callousness, arrogance, etc. are not pharmaceutically treatable. In the same way, there exists no medication, and likely never will, to create an operating capacity for empathy in psychopathic individuals.

If not "curable," can psychopathy be controlled in ways that might allow individuals to function successfully in the workplace? Recent work by behavioral economists, cognitive scientists, and psychologists (see Ariely, 2012, for a good summary of this work) has indicated that in addition to traditional incentive-based motivators for curbing undesirable behavior in the workplace like cheating and fraud, we are subject to two other very powerful psychological forces that have the effect of regulating our unethical behavior: (1) our sense of self, in particular our sense of ourselves as good, honest people, and (2) social norms. Research shows that even when faced with the opportunity to cheat maximally, we generally don't, instead cheating just a little bit. Ariely attributes this to our willingness to "fudge" on our sense of ourselves as good, honest individuals just a little bit each time, but not enough to threaten that self-image. We also respond to social cues or norms that signal to us whether particular forms of behavior are acceptable to the groups or communities we identify with. When faced situationally with such signals, we tend to refrain from such proscribed behavior. This work has direct implications for workplace management in that it provides another, in many cases more effective, approach to arranging the work environment in ways to control the extent of unethical behavior that occurs. If we allow that psychopathic personalities suffer from an ADA-covered disability that, if unaccommodated, would keep them from performing their job functions without posing a direct threat to themselves or others, and we recognize that appropriately tailored changes to the work environment in line with this research (e.g., providing constant reminders of an organization's core values to employees) could lessen that risk, then it could be at least argued that these work environment changes qualify as an accommodation that employers may be obligated to provide. Unfortunately, techniques for controlling workplace behavior that rely on appeals to an individual's sense of self or to social norms will be ineffective when it comes to psychopathic employees. Since they do not see the behavior they engage in as unethical in the first place, the opportunity to engage in self-serving behavior that harms others will not trigger their internal "fudge factor" because they don't have one. Likewise, since psychopathic individuals could care less about social expectations, social norm signaling will go unreceived. Because of this, it would be impossible to alter the work environment

One study has indicated that a reward-based treatment program can effectively help to manage psychopathic personalities in institutional settings by keeping them calm (Rogers et al., 2008), but there is no evidence that such a treatment program would translate to noninstitutional settings, such as a business organization. It is not, however, too much to consider that a reward-based treatment program could be translated into the workplace since much of the work environment is already incentive-based (e.g., raises, promotions, bonuses, etc.). As described in the previous chapter, Boddy has amassed data that indicates that Corporate Psychopaths are far more likely to engage in workplace bullying and other types of unjust treatment of coworkers. Appealing to the Corporate Psychopath's extreme egoism, an employer could, for example, put in place an incentive program that rewarded that individual in some way, say with financially appropriate bonuses, if they refrain from such behavior. Given that the Corporate Psychopath may be a valuable employee in other aspects of their work as described in the previous chapter, it may very well be in the employer's interest to figure out how to control the impact that the Corporate Psychopath's "negative" psychopathic traits could have on their ability to perform their job functions (assuming here that "job functions" understood broadly, as the ADA does, would include getting along with and not harming coworkers). The question is whether providing a "benefit" not provided to all employees would qualify as a "change to the workplace or work environment," and, hence, count as a reasonable accommodation. There is precedent for counting the provision of a reasonable amount of additional unpaid leave for medical treatment as a reasonable accommodation (Technical Assistance Manual, subsection 3.5), which could be construed as a benefit. So, there is some reason to think the "be good bonus" would qualify, but apart from an actual judicial review of a case involving a request for such an accommodation, it cannot be determined whether the reasonable accommodation requirement would extend this far.

SOME RECONSIDERATIONS

Considering the nature of psychopathy and the explicit requirements for protection and accommodation under the ADA, a substantial case can be made that job applicants and employees with psychopathic personalities would be protected against employment discrimination in the ways the ADA designates, and they would be rightful candidates for workplace accommodations where effective accommodations could be made for their mental impairment and where such accommodations do not constitute an undue hardship for employers. As discussed above, the language of the ADA would allow for employers to test for psychopathy after a job offer has been made. However, a diagnosis of psychopathy cannot be used to rescind the offer unless doing so is "job-related or consistent with business necessity" or the applicant poses a "direct threat" to themselves or others in the workplace. The same requirement holds for testing of employees and the decision to terminate. The prospects for an employer being able to make a good case that a psychopathic employee is unable to perform both incidental and essential job functions are good. The prospects of basing the decision to rescind an offer or fire an employee diagnosed as psychopathic are not as good given the emerging concerns about the reliability and validity of the PCL-R and other psychopathy screening instruments. Thus, even though a substantial case can be made that psychopathic personalities would be protected against discrimination in employment by the ADA, employers may still have some leeway to appeal to the provisions of the ADA to "weed out" Corporate Psychopaths. Nonetheless, there is something counterintuitive about the conclusion that Corporate Psychopaths, given the nature of their disorder and the harm they can potentially cause to others, should qualify for ADA protection in the first place. Is it plausible to believe that the original intent and purpose behind the crafting of the ADA would allow for a sensible extension of coverage to psychopathic personalities, even though strictly understood, the ADA's language might not allow for such an extension of coverage?

A reading of the purpose of the ADA provides a broader context in which to judge whether the intent of the ADA would accommodate protection for psychopathic personalities. In the "Findings and Purpose" statement of the ADA, the framers of the ADA provide a more detailed account of the intent behind the ADA (ADA, section 12101). There they describe both the reasons for enacting federal legislation to protect the disabled from discrimination (e.g., at the time of the drafting of the ADA the number of disabled Americans was approximately 43 million and growing, and "historically, society has tended to isolate and segregate individuals with disabilities," and "unlike individuals who have experienced discrimination on the basis of race, color, sex, national origin, religion, or age, individuals who have experienced discrimination on the basis of disability have often had no legal recourse to redress such discrimination") and the purpose of the ADA (i.e., "to provide clear, strong, consistent, enforceable standards addressing discrimination against individuals with disabilities" through the exercise of "the sweep of congressional authority, including the power to enforce the fourteenth amendment and to regulate commerce, in order to address the major areas of discrimination faced day-to-day by people with disabilities"). It is clear that the ADA is designed to address historical and ongoing discrimination endured by the disabled. It can be inferred from this that the individuals imagined by Congress to be the proper recipients of the benefit of protection against discrimination provided by the ADA are those who belong to groups who have been discriminated against or are at risk of discrimination. Taking this into account, it is difficult to imagine Corporate Psychopaths belonging to a group of individuals historically discriminated against or a group that is at risk of being subject to discrimination as things currently stand. Further, of importance for the claim that psychopathy *should* count as a disability under the ADA, is the following statement regarding the types of discrimination against the disabled the ADA is targeting: "discrimination against individuals with disabilities [that] persists in such critical areas as employment, housing, public accommodations, education, transportation, communication, recreation, institutionalization, health services, voting, and access to public services." Again, there is no historical record of psychopathic persons, as a group, being discriminated against in these areas up to the present time. The *potential* for pre-employment and post-hire screening for psychopathy *to give rise to* discrimination in an area like employment, a serious issue, will be addressed in more detail in the following chapter, but that is a forward-looking concern. The ADA addresses only historical and ongoing discrimination. One could argue that including psychopathic personalities in the category of the "disabled" as defined by the ADA is an unreasonable interpretation of the ADA.

As described previously, the ADA, as interpreted by the EEOC, does include "personality disorder" as a covered disability. Also, the EEOC Guidelines note that courts defer to the *DSM* for determinations of what is and what is not a personality disorder. As explained in chapter one, strictly speaking, "psychopathy" is not a personality disorder according to the *DSM*. Given the long history of the authors of the various editions of the *DSM* intentionally avoiding characterizing psychopathy as a clinically diagnosable personality disorder, a clinically "tight" reading of the ADA would not count psychopathy as a covered disability, and if the EEOC is correct about courts deferring to the *DSM* regarding what is and what is not a personality disorder, one would not expect a court to validate a claim that one had been discriminated against *because* of their psychopathy. Antisocial personality disorder, of which "psychopathy" is but a "specifier," would be covered, but not psychopathy per se. As described in chapter one, the long-reigning dispute regarding the *DSM*'s omission of "psychopathy" as a clinically recognized diagnosis is partly grounded in the distinction made between behavioral traits and personality traits. ASPD focuses primarily on behaviors (e.g., lying, deception, and manipulation for personal gain or amusement, impulsive behavior, aggression, and engaging in behavior that results in criminal arrest). If a diagnosis of ASPD refers to personality traits, it does so only secondarily. Psychopathy, on the other, is intentionally focused on personality traits. The PCL-R is designed as a diagnostic tool to identify the presence of personality traits like pathological egocentricity, absence of empathy, shame and regret, and superficial charm, and to, most importantly, diagnose the strength of those traits in individuals. A diagnosis of ASPD would be a diagnosis of a propensity to engage in certain forms of related behaviors, while a "diagnosis" of psychopathy would be a finding that an individual possessed a robust constellation of personality traits. An individual could be clinically diagnosed as having ASPD without having the personality traits specific to psychopathy, or at least not having those personality traits to the extent that would justify a finding of psychopathy. Consequently, it could be argued, an individual would not be able to claim psychopathy as a disability under the ADA, though, if it were true that they "also" were suffering from ASPD, they could under that *DSM*-recognized designation.

It must also be acknowledged that there is, at least on first read, an inconsistency in the argument developed in this chapter. On the one hand, the argument is that the ADA, since it covers mental impairments that include psychiatric disorders, would cover psychopathy and hence protect psychopathic personalities from discrimination in the hiring process. An employer could not require submission to a psychological screen like the PCL-R as part of the application process. Post conditional job offer and before the start of work, however, employers are allowed to administer medical examinations under the ADA as long as such exams objectively establish the fact of "significant current risk of substantial harm" if the applicant is actually hired and placed in the workplace. If this condition were met, then it could be argued that an employer could administer a medical examination intended to test for the presence of a psychopathic personality in the person of the applicant to whom the job offer has been extended. Uncertainty was cast on this conclusion due to the presence of doubt about the reliability and validity of the current psychological screening instruments that would most likely be the medical examination used as regards psychopathy. If such instruments cannot reliably identify the presence of a psychopathic personality nor validly establish that the risk employing psychopathic personalities is *significant*, then they would not qualify as acceptable medical examinations and could not be used. Even at the post-offer stage, psychopathic personalities would be protected from having to pass a medical examination to begin work. The inconsistency would seem to be this: psychopathic personalities would be covered under the ADA but, since there is no reliable or valid way to determine that job applicants possess a psychopathic personality, psychopathic job applicants would never be the target of hiring discrimination because they cannot be identified in the first place, unless they voluntarily offer up that they have a psychopathic personality during the application or interview processes. Their protection and right to workplace accommodations is based on their mental disability being identified and known, something that the argument later casts doubt on.

One way to clear up this *prima facie* inconsistency is to recognize that the reference to the uncertain status of the reliability and validity of current psychopathy screening instruments is intended to show only that their use would not pass ADA muster and, hence, even if an employer had other reasons for believing that an applicant to whom a job offer has been extended is in possession of a psychopathic personality, said employer could not under the ADA require that the applicant undergo *that particular medical examination* even if the other standards for requiring such an examination are met. There is a conditionality to this part of the argument, a temporal conditionality. Current psychopathy screening tools may not pass ADA muster, but this is not to say that future ones will not. If future screening tools, or current ones adequately revised, would be sufficiently reliable and valid, and the other conditions for requiring a post-offer medical examination are met, then they may be allowable under the ADA.

Also, the argument can be broken down into two parts: discrimination during the application process and discrimination post-offer. As noted above, given the current state of psychopathy screening instruments, it can be argued that they cannot be required as part of conditional job offers. The ADA would protect psychopathic personalities against that requirement. But, that is distinct from discrimination against psychopathic personalities during the hiring process preceding the extension of a job offer. Psychopathic personalities could still be subject to discrimination in the application and review portions of the overall hiring and onboarding process. For example, if an employer were interested in not hiring psychopathic personalities and was acquainted with even just the popular literature regarding psychopathy, interview questions could be arranged so as to "probe" for the presence of a psychopathic personality. Since such probing would not involve any "official" screening instruments, discrimination at this stage of the hiring process would not be tied to the reliability and validity of screening tools like the PCL-R; it would present independent of whether such screens tools are reliable and valid or not. Understood in this way, there is no actual inconsistency present in the argument that psychopathy could reasonably be seen as an ADA-covered disability.

Chapter Four

The Ethical Issues

The previous chapter makes the case for treating psychopathy as a "disability" under the Americans with Disabilities Act. As such, psychopathic personalities would be protected against discrimination in the hiring process and Corporate Psychopaths would be similarly protected in the workplace. Where efficacious and reasonable, employers would be obligated to provide accommodations for Corporate Psychopaths in their employ that would allow those employees to satisfactorily perform their job functions without posing a "direct threat" to themselves or others. A counterintuitive conclusion indeed, but one that seems to follow from a full reading of the ADA and accompanying EEOC documents. This conclusion, however, is a contingent one, as the ADA could always be amended again (it was amended in 2008 in response to a set of Supreme Court decisions interpreting the original text of the ADA) to *explicitly* exclude psychopathy as a covered disability if federal legislators chose to do so. Acknowledging the contingent status of the conclusion that psychopathy would be an ADA-covered "disability" and that legal scholars may yet weigh in to dispute the validity of that conclusion as it is defended in the previous chapter, the ethics of employment screening for psychopathy should be considered since it could become the case that such screening is not understood to be illegal discrimination, yet *is* recognized as unethical nonetheless. This chapter considers the latter case with the purpose of establishing the claim that employment screening for psychopathy runs the risk of violating principles of just treatment recognized as applicable in the areas of hiring and workforce management.

THE RELIABILITY AND VALIDITY OF THE PCL-R AND THE DENIAL OF EQUAL OPPORTUNITY

A concern for "equal opportunity" is not just a concern for political philosophy, where the claim to a right to full and equal participation in political practices and systems is generally regarded as a *sine qua non* of a "just" political community. At least in Western societies, the presence of a right of equal opportunity to participate fully in economic practices and institutions has also achieved the status of a necessary condition for a "just" economic community. Combining democracy and capitalism, the modern welfare state takes as its *reason d'etre* the promotion and protection of the well-being, economic and political, of its citizens. Institutions and practices that consistently deny equal opportunity to individuals and groups of individuals are anathema to that purpose. This is especially the case in the employment arena. Nations like the U.S. have enacted multiple pieces of legislation to curb unfair discrimination in the hiring process and in the workplace. What follows is an examination of the extent to which psychopathy screening, pre-employment and post-hire, may constitute a violation of this social commitment to the promotion and protection of the right to equal opportunity.

As noted in chapter one, Hare's PCL-R is generally regarded as the gold standard in diagnostic tools for identifying psychopathic personalities. Other tools, such as Boddy's PM-MRV, which makes use of a portion of the PCL-R and employee reports, and the B-Scan developed by Babiak and Hare, which has the same four-factor structure as the PCL-R, have been forwarded as substitutes for the use of the PCL-R in a corporate setting. As with all diagnostic tools used in psychology and psychiatry, the key concern is that the tools used are both "reliable" and "valid." In general, "reliability" refers to the consistency of the measurement instrument being used. There are two types of reliability, both important when considering the potential uses to which psychopathy-measuring diagnostic tests like the PCL-R would be put by employers. "Internal reliability" refers to the consistency of result across items within a measuring instrument, while "external reliability" refers to the consistency of results across multiple uses of the instrument. "External reliability" has two components: (1) consistency across time and (2) consistency across raters employing the instrument. Regarding the use of the PCL-R or other measuring instruments, to be reliable such instruments would have to produce similar PCL-R rater results when applied to the same individual or same group of individuals over time, and generate similar results when administered by different psychologists for the same individual or group of individuals. To be "valid," a test must be shown to actually measure what it is intended to measure. In the case of psychopathy screening, the PCL-R and other screening tests would need to actually identify psychopathic personality traits and not some other traits unrelated to a diagnosis of psychopathy, and to identify as "psychopaths" only those individuals for whom the possession of the relevant traits has risen to the level of a "disorder." Like all psychological tests, the PCL-R and similar instruments could be reliable without being valid (i.e., could produce consistent results but fail to measure what they are intended to measure). If the PCL-R or similar instruments lack either reliability or validity, then they have the potential to produce "false positives" and "false negatives." In the former case, psychopathy tests would label some subjects as "psychopaths" depending upon the rater involved when they would not be so identified by other raters or not identified as such if retested. For the latter case, psychopathy tests would fail to identify actual "psychopaths" for the same reasons. The first possibility, that false positives would be generated, raises the concern that the use of psychopathy screening instruments like the PCL-R for decision-making regarding employment could deny some individuals their right to equal opportunity and just treatment. The second possibility, that some actual psychopathic personalities would "slip through" the screening process and find a home in the workplace where they pose the various risks already described, undercuts the argument that psychopathy screening allows employers to satisfy their legitimate business interests in creating a safe, nonhostile workplace and in protecting the organization against legal liability and financial malfeasance. Both possible outcomes make the use of such instruments ethically troublesome. As early as 2006, Babiak and Hare acknowledged that "underreporting" and "overreporting" of the numbers of Corporate Psychopaths actually present is a real problem that would plague attempts to establish a scientific basis for the Corporate Psychopath Hypothesis, due to their ability to elude detection, in the case of "underreporting," and due to the fact that psychopathy is a dimensional construct, in the case of "overreporting" (Babiak & Hare, 2006).

Early testing of the PCL-R in controlled research settings indicated moderate to strong interrater reliability and predictive validity (Gacono & Hutton, 1994; Grann et al., 1998; and Cooke et al., 2004). In his "manual" on the PCL-R, Hare reports findings defending the reliability and predictive validity of his namesake screening instrument (Hare, 2003). In some field studies conducted in North America during the last decade, however, the PCL-R has shown less reliability. In a review of cases involving sexually violent predators and the use of the PCL–R, less than half of the cases containing multiple PCL-R scores per individual fell within one standard error of measurement unit (DeMatteo et al., 2014). In a sample of 102 Canadian criminal cases containing multiple PCL-R scores for offenders, Edens et al. (2015) reported that for those cases the standard error of measurement was much larger than that reported in Hare's manual. A second study of Canadian court cases, this one involving 136 dangerous offender hearings, found that PCL-R scores assigned to offenders varied with trial outcomes (Lloyd et al., 2010). Supportive of an emerging theory that PCL-R raters are influenced by their professional allegiance within an adversarial setting (i.e., they are supporting witnesses for the defense or for the prosecution), Murrie, et al. (2009) reviewed sexual offender civil commitment cases in which opposing evaluators reported PCL-R scores for the same individual. They found that differences between scores from opposing evaluators were often greater than expected based on rater agreement values reported in Hare's manual and in research literature. In 2017, Jeandarme et al. published the results of their study of archived clinical PCL-R scores of a forensic psychiatric sample of 224 Belgian offenders found "not guilty by reason of insanity" and classified as medium security risks (Jeandarme et al., 2017). The offenders were tested originally in a prison setting or in a hospital setting, or in both for a subset of the sample. In 48 cases (21% of the overall sample) multiple PCL-R scores were available. They found that,

> [t]he general conclusion of the current study in this sample of forensic psychiatric patients was that the PCL-R in real world settings conducted by real world raters in Belgium is fairly unreliable although there was some evidence of modest to moderate predictive validity for Factor 2 scores. These results are generally consistent with a growing body of field research suggesting that the high levels of reliability reported in many controlled research studies are not generalizable to practice settings. (Jeandarme et al., p. 37)

In particular, they found that there was consistency in the ratings of offenders within the prison setting and within the hospital setting, but when the scores from different settings for the same offenders were compared, they found that the mean prison scores were lower than mean hospital scores (Jeandarme et al., 2017). They attribute the low reliability to differences in the contexts where testing was administered (e.g., due to a shortage of beds in high security hospital facilities, prison raters were under pressure to score inmates lower so that they could be transferred to a medium security facility) and to differences in the raters themselves (e.g., education).

Regarding predictive validity, Jeandarme et al. found that "only the total and Facet 3 hospital scores significantly predicted general recidivism, whereas none of the scores reached significance for violent recidivism" (Jeandarme et al., p. 39). These findings are consistent with those generated by Neal, Miller, and Shealy (2015) in a study of archival data (sample size of 230) of a prerelease violence risk assessment battery administered over 6 years at a forensic hospital. The battery of tests used to generate the original assessments of risk of recidivism included the PCL-R. They found that the battery of assessments failed to predict recidivism better than chance. Similarly, a meta-analysis of sexual reoffending by Hawes, Boccaccini, and Murrie (2013) found that the predictive validity for sexual recidivism differed significantly depending upon whether the rater was a researcher or a clinician, indicating that an absence of interrater reliability was connected to low predictive validity.

Boddy's PM-MRV has similarly been criticized for lacking in predictive validity (Jones & Hare, 2016). In the case of the PM-MRV, the charge that it lacks predictive validity is based on how the PM-MRV constructs its measure of psychopathic traits. As described in chapter one, the PCL-R makes reference to four "correlated dimensions" or "first-order factors" in its measure of psychopathic traits: (1) *Interpersonal* (e.g., glibness/superficial charm, grandiose sense of self-worth, and pathological lying), (2) *Affective* (e.g., lack of remorse or guilt, lack of empathy, and failure to take responsibility for actions), (3) *Lifestyle* (e.g., need for stimulation to relieve boredom, and impulsivity), and (4) *Antisocial* (e.g., poor behavioral controls and early behavioral problems related to criminality). The construct of "psychopathy" as measured by the PCL-R is a superordinate one composed of patterns of correlation among these four first-order factors. In their commentary on Boddy's PM-MRV, in addition to asking about its originality given its use of two of the first-order factors from the PCL-R, Jones and Hare focus on the role that employee reports of like/dislike of their coworker or supervisor may play in generating PM-MRV scores indicative of a psychopathic personality. Drawing upon the results of two sample surveys of working individuals on Amazon's Mechanical Turk, they found that "simply disliking one's supervisor accounted for 63% of the total PM-MRV variance," and, hence, "it appears that the PM-MRV measures how much individuals like their supervisors," not whether their supervisors are actually "psychopaths" (Jones & Hare, 2015, pp. 582–583). Additionally, as they argue, since the PM-MRV uses only the Factor 1 traits from the PCL-R, it fails to distinguish between the presence of psychopathy and the other "dark personalities," such as Machiavellianism and narcissism, noticeably lessening its predictive validity. They draw the following general summary of the usefulness of the PM-MRV in identifying "corporate psychopaths."

> Disentangling psychopathy, narcissism, Machiavellianism, and other dark personalities is critical to advancing research on corporate harm. The PM-MRV may assess only features common to these dark personalities and therefore cannot provide essential information about how they differ with respect to their nature, the strategies they use, and their dispositions toward corporate misbehavior. As a research tool, the PM-MRV is not specific with respect to psychopathy

and provides misleading information about the role of the PCL-R psychopathy construct in the business world. (Jones & Hare, 2015, p. 585)

As for the B-Scan, a search of *PsycARTICLES* and *PsycINFO*, the two databases supported by the American Psychological Association, shows only a single article that addresses the reliability and validity of the instrument, and that article is authored by Hare and colleagues (Mathieu et al., 2013). This is insufficient evidence to determine whether the B-Scan avoids the interrater reliability and predictive validity issues that emerging research is identifying with the PCL-R. It would be surprising if those issues did not also surface with the B-Scan given that it is built on the exact same four-factor structure as the PCL-R. Further, given that it is intended to be used by human resources professionals in the business setting, the finding of Jeandarme et al. that PCL-R scores can be influenced to a significant degree by the education of the rater and the kind and extent of training they have had, it is reasonable to expect that such professionals would fall on the lower end of the scale in terms of knowledge and training adequate to making reliable and valid judgments about individuals subjected to the B-Scan as part of the hiring process or as part of employee review processes. At best, the jury is still out on the reliability and predictive validity of this modified version of the PCL-R.

Given the frequency with which the PCL-R is used in mental health evaluations in criminal cases, especially in the sentencing phase, an absence of instrument reliability and predictive validity means that fair or just resolutions to such cases may not be reached. The emerging realization that the PCL-R does not perform as well as advertised in field settings creates justice concerns regarding its use in the employment setting, a type of field setting as well. The use of the PCL-R or other screening instruments necessarily involves some subjective judgment on the part of the raters administering the test and interpreting the responses. This allows for the possibility that raters' judgements can be influenced by external pressures and by the settings in which they are asked to provide judgments. As noted above, there is some evidence that raters may score criminal offenders differently depending upon whether they are "working for" the prosecution or the defense in that they may feel obligated in some way to produce judgments that suit the role their testimony plays in the court proceedings (researchers call this "adversarial allegiance"). Similarly, as Jeandarme et al. have shown, system pressures such as the need to move convicted offenders more quickly out of the prison setting into a psychiatric hospital setting may influence the PCL-R score raters assign. When interrater subjectivity exceeds reasonable limits, an anchor principle of justice is violated. A foundational principle of justice requires impartiality in judgment making. It is a demand for procedural justice. Similar cases should be treated similarly, not differently based on the particular interests or biases of the individual or institution making the judgments. The rule of law is intended to capture this justice commitment by requiring that said rules be applied impartially over time. The lack of interrater reliability also threatens to produce results that violate a principle of substantive justice: the principle that individuals should receive what they are properly due. In the case of criminal cases, that principle would require that offenders receive the proper sentencing outcome that fits their crime. If sentencing decisions are based on psychopathy diagnoses generated by the use of the PCL-R, the lack of interrater reliability would mean that some offenders receive unjust sentencing outcomes. Would these concerns for justice and psychopathy screening extend to the employment setting?

A concern for equal opportunity, a type of the more general justice concern for equal treatment, is grounded in the interests that members of any community, be it one organized politically or economically, in having access to those positions, roles, activities, etc. that confer benefits on those participating in them. Rawls (1999) captures this concern in his second basic principles of justice, the "Difference Principle": Social and economic inequalities are to be arranged so that they are both: (a) to the greatest benefit of the least advantaged, consistent with the just savings principle, and (b) attached to offices and positions open to all under conditions of fair equality of opportunity. Rawls's take on the just distribution of goods, services, and access is that it does not require an absolutely equal distribution, in contrast to his view on the distribution of basic liberties, which must be egalitarian. Instead, inequalities in this area can be claimed to be just if the two conditions are met. Arbitrary barriers to attainment of those offices and positions that enjoy the upper end of the inequality relationships they are a part of (e.g., inequality in salaries attached to different occupations) are deemed unjust because if the participants in a system that they know may distribute benefits and advantages differentially are "veiled" to the particular place in such system they will occupy, they would opt for a rule of justice that requires there be no barriers to attainment of offices and positions that are not merit-based.

If psychopathy screening were to become common practice, then job applicants who score above a certain threshold on the PCL-R (and that threshold would not necessarily have to be the score of 30 that identifies one as possessed of a psychopathic personality, it could be lower than that) would be excluded from accessing those offices and positions for which the screening is required. From the Rawlsian perspective, two concerns emerge regarding the ethics of this outcome. Recall the distinction that the EEOC guidelines for implementation of ADA requirements makes between "essential job functions," which are the reference point for making the "consistent with business necessity" argument, and "incidental job functions," which can be referenced in claiming the "job-related" exemption. For the most part, if one is focused on the formal and technical job functions laid out in the typical job description, it is not likely that the possession of heightened psychopathic traits would inhibit a job applicant's ability to perform these functions. A psychopathic person can be a "good" accountant, a "good" marketing director, a "good" warehouse worker, a "good" CEO, etc., in the sense that they are quite able to perform the explicit, technical requirements of those positions. Referring back to Dutton's claims about the capabilities of psychopathic personalities, there are some jobs for which psychopathic individuals are "well suited." Using the language of the ADA, there is no reason to believe that psychopathic personalities cannot perform "essential job functions" for most occupations. Since most explicit and implicit employment contracts, based as they are on job descriptions, are heavily slanted toward "essential functions," excluding individuals who are otherwise qualified from accessing jobs because of their psychopathic profile counts as an arbitrary barrier, and would, consequently, violate Rawls's Difference Principle. It would be a denial of their right to equal opportunity, a right that the ADA itself is intended to protect. Things are not quite as straightforward if the argument shifts to consider the use of "job-related, incidental functions" as a merit-based qualification for access to employment. As discussed in the previous chapter, if the ability to treat coworkers respectfully is considered an incidental job function and the ability to successfully perform incidental job functions can be understood to be part of any employment contract, then the systematic exclusion of psychopathic personalities from the workplace would not be an arbitrary barrier. This would only apply to those jobs that involve sustained interaction with coworkers. So, for example, jobs that can be performed remotely or ones that require very little interaction with coworkers, say working in a call center, would not be ethically legitimate candidates for "job-related" exemptions from the requirements of Rawls's Difference Principle. At best, it could be claimed for only a subset of jobs that psychopathy screening does not present an arbitrary, and, hence, unjust barrier to equal opportunity of access to employment.

Yet, even this qualified conclusion is undermined from a Rawlsian justice perspective by the emerging evidence that the PCL-R and other screening instruments lack sufficient reliability and predictive validity. It is reasonable to suspect that professionals hired to conduct psychopathy screening for employers using these instruments will experience an "allegiance" to that employer very similar to the kind of "adversarial allegiance" cited by researchers examining the interrater reliability and predictive validity of uses of the PCL-R in criminal court cases. They will feel a heightened sense of responsibility to be "thorough" in their assessments, since to misidentify an applicant to whom a job offer has been extended would create liability for the employer and put the employer's business enterprise at risk of harm. As in the criminal court setting, raters will seek to satisfy the interests of their employers and likely err on the side of caution by "overrating" in their assessment of applicants to whom job offers have been tendered. In effect, the chances of false positives being generated are significant. This would mean that due to rater bias, individuals who have otherwise been deemed the best candidates for a job, since an offer has been extended, will be arbitrarily denied the opportunity.

A basic commitment of a just society in all areas political and economical is to ensure that its members' right to equal opportunity, which includes the right to not have arbitrary barriers in place that keep them from participating fully in the political and economic practices necessary for the attainment of personal well-being, is not abridged by circumstance or the arbitrary decisions of others. The argument of this section is that if psychopathy screening of job applicants to whom offers have been made and of current employees were to be made use of by employers, just such an abridgment would occur. In the absence of substantial reason to believe that Corporate Psychopaths are, because of their "disorder," incapable of performing the essential functions of their job, screening them out based on a diagnosis of psychopathy would be arbitrary and a denial of equal opportunity. Even if the case can be made that it is reasonable for an employer to be wary of hiring or retaining psychopathic individuals because of their inability to interact with others respectfully, an incidental job function, the serious questions that recent research has raised about the reliability and predictive validity of the psychological tests that most likely would be used by employers indicate that the likelihood of psychopathic screening in the employment arena producing consistent false positives is unacceptably high. To be labelled a "psychopath" as part of the pre-employment process or as part of employee review processes based on unreliable and non-predictive testing would, as well, be an abridgement of the right to equal opportunity of those denied employment access because of the results of the testing.

PSYCHOPATHY SCREENING AND PRIVACY

Though not invasive in the same way or to the same extent as bodily surgery, being subjected to psychopathy testing is invasive in that the subject's psychology is being probed, and probed to a significant depth in that tests like the PCL-R are intended to reveal to the administer of the test not only superficial psychological traits, knowledge of which could be gained from simple observation, but also "deeper" psychological traits that potentially enable or disable behavioral traits. As described in chapter one, the ongoing dispute around whether or not the *DSM* should include "psychopathy" as a distinct, clinical diagnosis is substantially a dispute about whether behavioral traits alone are sufficient for a diagnosis of the kind of mental disorder "psychopathy" is intended to designate. Psychologists supportive of including "psychopathy" as a distinct type of mental disorder believe not. It is their belief that psychopathy involves the presence of a constellation of psychological traits that, if present to a heightened degree, mark one as a psychopathic personality, whether or not one has yet to engage in psychopathic behavior (e.g., as in found with "functioning psychopaths"). "Psychopathy" is a designation of a distinct psychological profile, not of behavioral patterns. As such, testing for it requires an in-depth probing of a subject's psyche for the presence of those traits. In the language of the ethics of privacy, psychopathy testing constitutes an "intrusion" into that part of ourselves, our psyche, which we typically treat as private. Because of this, and due to the fact that our default position on the ethics of privacy is that intrusions need proper ethical justification, the proposal for pre-employment and post-hire psychopathy screening raises significant ethical issues.

In their excellent treatment of the ethical implications of forms of workplace testing, such as drug testing and genetic testing, for an employee's *prima facie* right to privacy, Persson and Hansson (2003) develop an account of what "privacy" means, what arguments an employer might offer for intruding into employee privacy, and what criteria must be met for any such intrusions to be ethically justified. Their approach is a good model to use to examine the potential that psychopathy screening has to be a privacy violation because the model is designed to specifically address an employer's interest in obtaining information about employees that cannot be readily obtained from simple observation and to outline the limitations that should be in place for the pursuit of that interest so as to properly respect an employee's ethical expectation of privacy (all of which is easily extended to pre-employment screening). Two of the three employer interests they consider match the employer interests that lay behind arguments for psychopathy screening described in chapter two. As they note, "[t]he employer can argue (1) that his/her own (business) interests justifies intrusions into workers' privacy, (2) that it is justified by the interests of the employee, or (3) that it is justified as a means to protect a interested third party's legitimate interests" (Persson & Hansson, 2003, p. 65). The "reduction of organizational risk" argument cited for psychopathy screening lines up with the "business interests" justification for privacy intrusions, and the "prevention of harm and unjust treatment" argument as well as the "protection of social/economic systems" argument are clear examples of the "protection of a third party's interests" justification for intruding into the privacy of employees and job applicants.

Persson and Hansson acknowledge that discussions of privacy are really only of interest if the concept of "privacy" has normative force, meaning that treating "privacy" as a value, something to be protected, is to imply that it has ethical significance. Otherwise, discussions of "privacy" would be purely descriptive and imply no restrictions on the freedom of others to access the information that would fall into the category of the "private." The most common way to capture this normative force is to identify a right to privacy. This right, however, is only a *prima facie* right, not an absolute one, because we can reasonably justify violations of this right (e.g., a court can subpoena information or evidence that we would consider to be private information). They offer the following way of conceptualizing privacy as a normative concern:

1. A statement that X is a matter of A's privacy is or implies a prima facie normative claim that access to X should be limited in the interest of A. It follows that infringements of privacy always need a justification.
2. What counts as matters of privacy is the outcome of social norms and ideals, and may be different in different cultures.
3. An individual's sphere of privacy (i.e., the collection of matters to which (s)he has legitimate privacy claims, consists of two parts: (a) The core, that consists of such privacy rights that others should respect whether (s)he claims them or not, and (b) the discretionary part that consists of the privacy rights that others have to respect only if (s)he claims them (Persson & Hansson, 2003, pp. 62–63).

They divide the sphere of privacy into two parts, a *core* and a *discretionary* part (Persson & Hansson, 2003). The core consists of that information that will always be considered private information whether or not an individual cares if others access or know the information. Their example is a person's casebook from a stay in a mental hospital. Said person could adopt the attitude of not caring if others access the information contained in the casebook, but this attitude does not change the nature of the information as private, it only reflects the stance the subject of the information has taken regarding others accessing the information. The discretionary part covers that information that is to be regarded as private *only if* the subject of the information actually seeks to maintain it as such. Their example is a person with a chest scar who makes no effort to hide the scar from the sight of others. Whether the information that they have a chest scar is to be regarded as private is entirely a function of the attitude the person with the scar adopts regarding it. Their conceptualization of what is a matter of privacy is a culturally relative one in the sense that expectations as to how others will treat information about oneself are the product of socially determined norms, not the result of an application of universal principles. This stance on the source of normative privacy expectations is not a worry for the present discussion of psychopathy screening and privacy because, if need be, this discussion can be restricted to Western societies, without loss of relevancy, where it is a well-regarded social norm that information about a person's mental health is considered to be private information.

As noted above, the employer interests at the center of arguments supportive of psychopathy screening are examples of the types of employer interests that Persson and Hansson consider as premising arguments for justifying intrusions into employee privacy. They present the following four criteria as necessary requirements for any such intrusions to be ethically justified:

1. The intrusion is undertaken with one of the following three purposes:
   (a) to ensure that the employee performs the tasks and fulfils the role responsibilities, owed to the employer, that are explicit or implicit in the contract of employment,
   (b) to protect the employee's own interests in matters for which the employer is morally responsible, and to do this with means that are also in the employee's own interest, or
   (c) to protect a third party's legitimate interests in matters for which the employer is morally responsible.
2. The intrusion is performed in a way that is an efficient means to achieve its purpose.
3. The intrusion is performed with the least intrusive means that are available to achieve its purpose.
4. The resulting intrusion into the employee's privacy is not so severe as to outweigh the value of achieving its purpose (Persson and Hansson, 2003, p. 68).

Would pre-employment and post-hire screening for psychopathy satisfy these four criteria? Let's begin with the "purposes" set of conditions. Is knowledge of the psychopathic traits of a potential employee or current employee necessary to ensure that an employee is able to "perform the tasks and fulfill the role responsibilities owed to the employer that are explicit or implicit in the contract of employment?" As noted above in the section on equal opportunity, for the most part, it is not likely that the possession of heightened psychopathic traits would inhibit an employee's ability to perform their job functions as required by the employment contract. Psychopathic persons can be, and often are (recall Dutton's claims about the "wisdom of psychopaths"), capable of excelling in the execution of their jobs. Knowledge of an employee's "psychopathic status," therefore, is unnecessary for an employer to ensure that an employee is capable of performing the tasks and role responsibilities defined in their employment contract. As such, seeking out such knowledge could not be claimed as a legitimate purpose under Persson and Hansson's schema. If the breadth of "the contract of employment" is widened to include *all* possible functions associated with a job *as set out by the employer*, whether or not they are explicitly identified in the contract, then the employer claim to need to know about the psychopathic status of job applicants and current employees may qualify as a legitimate purpose for intruding into the privacy of those individuals. To allow this, however, is to place the argument on a slippery slope because it opens up for discussion a slew of other options employers might pursue to gain knowledge of an individual's ability to treat others respectfully, which is the concern with psychopathic employees. What, it could be argued, would preclude an employer from hiring a private detective to follow employees around as they go through their daily lives secretly recording their activities for evidence of "sociability?" The point here is that if employers are allowed to, in effect, decide themselves what count as "incidental job functions," and such functions qualify as part of the overall set of tasks and role responsibilities understood to be in the contract of employment, then it is quite unclear what information about job applicants or employees would be ethically "out of bounds."

A safe workplace is something that employees are interested in and we generally hold employers responsible for protecting their employees from harm in the workplace. Given the evidence that Corporate Psychopaths have the potential to cause recognizable physical and mental harms to coworkers, the second "purpose" for intruding into the privacy of employees and potential employees would seem to be satisfied. For a strong claim to be made that this criterion is satisfied, however, the data actually linking Corporate Psychopaths to workplace harm to self and others would need to be more robust than currently exists. Allowing that the research that does exist is on the right track, and if researchers and clinicians were allowed greater access to test employees routinely causing workplace harm, an appeal to this criterion as the purpose psychopathy screening is intended to serve will still face questions about the predictive validity of the likely assessment measure to be used in serving that purpose. In the previous chapter, the extent to which an employer could avail themselves of the ADA-defined "direct threat" justification (the individual to be screened poses a risk to the safety and health of self or others) for psychopathy screening was examined. The conclusion drawn was that, though it makes perfect sense to regard Corporate Psychopaths as posing a "direct threat" to themselves and others, due to issues regarding the reliability and predictive validity of the PCL-R, the B-Scan, and the PM-MRV, issues that have been covered more extensively in this chapter, and the ADA requirement that the judgment that a job applicant *would be* or the judgment that a current employee *is* a "direct threat" be based on "objective medical or other factual evidence regarding the particular individual," it is unlikely that employers would be able to as common practice screen for psychopathy in an effort to minimize the existence of "direct threats" in the workplace. The same reasoning and conclusion drawn in the previous chapter can be extended to the claim that psychopathy screening is an ethically justified intrusion into employee (or potential employee) privacy based on those employee interests for which an employer has moral responsibility. If the "gold standard" for identifying psychopathic personalities lacks predictive validity, then the claim that psychopathic screening allows employers to satisfy their moral responsibility falls short.

An identical conclusion can be drawn regarding Persson and Hansson's third "purpose" for intruding into employee privacy. It is not in question that Corporate Psychopaths have the potential to cause physical and mental suffering to those they come into contact with, which would include not just coworkers but also third parties such as employees from other firms that they interact with. For an appeal to this third "purpose" to be substantive and not primarily speculative, which, if it were the case, would not be adequate to ethically justify a privacy intrusion, it must be reasonable to expect that Corporate Psychopaths will be a "direct threat." Considering the purported existence of "functioning psychopaths" and the emerging evidence casting doubt on the predictive validity of the PCL-R and other screening instruments, it has yet to be definitively established that the presence of psychopathic personalities in the workplace is a *real* risk. If Boddy's "Corporate Psychopaths Theory of the Global Financial Crisis" was to turn out to be correct, then the interests of third parties (i.e., members of those social and economic systems in which the institutions employing Corporate Psychopaths are embedded), have been impacted negatively by the presence of psychopathic employees, thereby providing historical support for an employer's appeal to this third "purpose." Boddy's theory, however, is purely speculative, based entirely on the belief that the modern corporation is a suitable environment for psychopathic personalities to flourish. No direct connections have yet to be made between *actual* psychopathic personalities at *actual* global financial firms having made *actual* decisions precipitating the financial crisis.

Persson and Hanson's second criterion, "the intrusion is performed in a way that is an efficient means to achieve its purpose," which must be satisfied no matter the purpose behind the intrusion, is categorically worrisome when considering psychopathy screening. The argument that psychopathy screening allows employers to satisfy a legitimate interest they have in ensuring that employees fulfill their job functions and other role responsibilities is a weak one if it is restricted to the ability to perform "essential job functions," since there is no reason to suspect that an employee with a psychopathic personality could not do that. If "tasks and role responsibilities" is expanded to include "incidental job functions," the ADA standard for "job-relatedness," then the case for psychopathy screening is stronger. The strength of the case for justifying the intrusion into employee privacy via psychopathy screening by appealing to an employer's responsibility to keep employees and third parties from harm is dependent upon the strength of the correlation between the rate of psychopathic personalities in the workplace and the incidents of workplace harm like bullying and unfair treatment. Much more data than is currently available is needed for this correlation to be more than speculative in nature. Also, doubts about the predictive validity of psychopathy screening instruments in forensic and clinical settings weaken the claim that psychopathic screening would actually be efficacious in aiding employers to satisfy their responsibility to prevent harm to employees and third parties. For each purpose, there is contingency that attaches to using it as a justification for psychopathy screening. For the second criterion, however, there is no contingency in judging the extent to which psychopathy meets the requirement. If the PCL-R and similar measurement instruments lack reliability and predictive validity, then they categorically are not "efficient means" to meet any of the three purposes for screening. This method of intruding into the mental health of employees cannot be considered efficient if it fails to consistently predict whether an employee will pose a "direct threat" to themselves or others, no matter the strength of the justification for intruding into employee privacy in this way. Additionally, the administration of the PCL-R, the B-Scan, or the PM-MRV is not a simple matter. Each test must be administered, the responses compiled in a way so as to calculate a score, and the results must be interpreted by the rater to provide a "psychopathic risk profile" that an employer can use in decision-making, all of which is aimed at providing evidence that an employer could confidently rely on. If there is a more straightforward method for generating evidence that employers could confidently rely on in making hiring and firing decisions, then they would be ethically bound to use that method.

Desjardins and Duska have commented on this exact scenario as regards employer use of drug testing (Desjardins & Duska, 2005). Treating drug testing as a *prima facie* violation of an employee's right to privacy, similar to Persson and Hansson, they consider the two main arguments given for drug testing: (1) An employer has a legitimate interest in employee productivity and drug use lowers employee productivity, and (2) Drug use often leads to harm and an employer has a legitimate interests in preventing harm in the workplace. Again, these same two arguments are mustered in defense of psychopathy screening. As for obtaining knowledge of employee drug use in order to ensure that employees are performing their jobs in line with employer expectations, Desjardins and Duska conclude that,

> If the person is producing what is expected, knowledge of drug use on the grounds of production is irrelevant since, by this hypothesis, the production is satisfactory. If, on the other hand, the performance suffers, then to the extent that it slips below the level justifiably expected, the employer has preliminary grounds for warning, disciplining, or releasing the employee. But the justification for this action is the person's unsatisfactory performance, not the person's drug use. Accordingly, drug use information is either unnecessary or irrelevant and consequently there are not sufficient grounds to override the right of privacy. (DesJardins & Duska, p. 223)

The same can be said of psychopathy information; it is either unnecessary because the employee is fulfilling their "tasks and role responsibilities" per the employment contract satisfactorily or it is irrelevant because the employee's failure to perform satisfactorily is itself sufficient ground for termination; there is no need to know that it is caused by the employee's psychopathic personality traits. Observation of the employee's work is a sufficient source of evidence for the decision to terminate and it is much more efficiently gathered than knowledge of the employee's psyche. Similarly, observations of employee behavior can reveal the presence of a risk for causing workplace harm, something that falls squarely within the job duties of management in supervisory roles. Before it reaches the level of workplace bullying, for example, attentive supervisors should be able to detect the risk for that in precursor behavior such as disrespectful speech and the creation of conflict, as well as from reports from coworkers (assuming that there is a working mechanism in place for employees to report disrespectful and threatening behavior). Such behavior alone constitutes sufficient grounds for dismissal, no need to know that it is the product of a psychopathic personality.

In summary, given the current state of research on the correlation between psychopaths in the workplace and workplace harm, and given the emerging evidence that the PCL-R and other psychopathy screens lack sufficient interrater reliability and predictive validity, psychopathy screening of job applicants and employees would constitute an unethical intrusion into the privacy of those individuals subjected to that screening. If the criteria Persson and Hansson set for ethically justifying intrusions into employees' presumed *prima facie* right to privacy are appropriate ones to require, which it has been claimed they are, then, given the right conditions, employers may be able to make a legitimate claim to access the information they would garner from psychopathy screening. However, the means by which they would presumably acquire that information, the application of the PCL-R test for example, would not meet the "efficient means" criteria in any case. This conclusion is bolstered by the fact that employers could acquire better information upon which to base a hiring or firing decision via other means that do not involve an admitted privacy violation.

UTILITARIAN CONSIDERATIONS

The common focus of the arguments for employment screening for psychopathy is on the harm that Corporate Psychopaths inflict on coworkers and the damage they do to organizational "health," or are likely to cause. Dutton's suggestion that Corporate Psychopaths may actually be of benefit to an organization in certain circumstances because their psychopathic personality traits may prove advantageous to the business interests of the organization, as was discussed in chapter two, can be used to defend employment screening for psychopathy as something an organization may have a positive, business interest in doing. If Dutton is right, then certain organizations may benefit from having Corporate Psychopaths in strategic positions. This possible benefit to the firm's business interests, even if substantiated and not just mere possibility, has to be weighed against the organizational harms that the presence of Corporate Psychopaths will likely produce. In effect, when the arguments based on the detrimental consequences of employing psychopathic personalities are considered along with the positive business interest argument, what we have is a utilitarian scenario: Do the benefits of having Corporate Psychopaths around outweigh the harms of doing so, even if only in certain cases? A utilitarian consideration such as this is moot if employees have a right to occupational safety and that right extends to protection from psychological and emotional harms. The function of rights, moral or civil, is to provide a shield from utilitarian calculations for their possessors. Using Kantian language, the possession of rights entails that individuals cannot be used as "mere means" as part of some social, business, or economic calculation of net benefits/costs. No amount of projected net benefit from doing so can justify overriding individual rights. To do so would be to violate the very nature of rights. Recognizing that, one could still be interested in the utilitarian comparison of the harms that Corporate Psychopaths create and the benefits they produce on the off chance that the destructive behavior of specific Corporate Psychopaths could be suppressed via external means or that, in some way, they are "functioning psychopaths" who are capable of self-suppression.

Strange as it may sound, there is some evidence that certain employees may actually benefit from working under Corporate Psychopaths. Hurst, Simon, Jung, and Pirouz argue that "high primary psychopathy individuals possess characteristics that enable them to experience higher levels of well-being and lower levels of anger than their peers under abusive supervisors" (Hurst et al., 2019, p. 1149). Based on two surveys conducted on a sample of 433 employed U.S. participants, they reported confirming evidence for three hypotheses:

Hypothesis 1: Abusive supervision moderates the relationship between primary psychopathy and positive affect such that primary psychopathy is positively related to positive affect under high levels of abusive supervision.

Hypothesis 2: Abusive supervision moderates the relationship between primary psychopathy and anger such that primary psychopathy is negatively related to anger under high levels of abusive supervision.

Hypothesis 3: Abusive supervision moderates the relationship between primary psychopathy and engagement such that primary psychopathy is positively related to engagement under high levels of abusive supervision.

This group of "bad employees" who positively benefit from abusive supervision would of necessity need to have their benefits be included in any utilitarian-style argument for Corporate Psychopath screening.

A consideration that bears upon the utilitarian argument is the extent to which the harmful behavior of Corporate Psychopaths could be curtailed. If, in at least some instances, Corporate Psychopaths bring some value to the organizations they work in, and their negative behavior could be curtailed through a disincentive, punishment-based program, then their presence might result in a net benefit. One problem for this line of reasoning is that psychopathic personalities do not experience fear in the same way that the rest of the population generally does. In 1957, Lykken studied the anxiety response of individuals with psychopathic personalities as compared to the anxiety response of non-psychopathic individuals (Lykken, 1957). A test group composed of "non-psychopaths" and persons with psychopathic personalities were repeatedly exposed to a sound followed by an electric shock. The "non-psychopath" group developed the typical states of anxiety and tension one would expect them to develop in response to hearing the sound. The group with psychopathic personalities, on the other hand, displayed only moderate levels of anxiety, which lasted for only a brief moment. More recent work has shown that while "the evidence for reduced subjective experience of fear in psychopathy is far less compelling," there is stronger evidence that "psychopathic individuals have deficits in threat detection and responsivity" (Hoppenbrouwers et al., 2016, p. 573). Such deficits would likely entail that a punishment-based deterrence system would not effectively curtail the harmful behavior that Corporate Psychopaths tend to engage in. This conclusion is supported by a study reported out by Siegel in the late 1970s (Siegel, 1978). He studied a group of 50 patients at a treatment center for individuals with a criminal history of sexual offense. The 50 patients were divided evenly into two groups: (1) those scoring below the median on a measure of psychopathy using items from Cleckley's checklist, and (2) those scoring above the median. Subjects were asked to turn over cards one at a time from a series of decks of cards. If a numbered card was drawn, they would receive a chip. If a face card was drawn, they would lose a chip. The decks had varied numbers of numbered cards and face cards (some had many more numbered cards than face cards, some had many more face cards, etc.). Subjects could choose to stop turning over cards from the current deck at any point, and move on to the next deck. After subjects had gone through the card turning process for all ten decks, they were told they would be able to "cash out" their chips. At two points during the card-turning exercise, subjects were asked to estimate the chances that the next card, if turned over, would be a "punishment card." Their "suppression rate" was a function of the number of cards they left unturned in each deck, on average. The results indicated that the psychopathic patient group showed less suppression of behavior in the face of possible punishment (i.e., turning over a face card next) than the non-psychopathic group, especially when the probability of punishment was not certain. This finding was consistent with that reported on by Hare in 1970 (Hare, 1970).

Clarke has expressed suspicion of the Dutton suggestion that there is a possibility of an overall net benefit from employing Corporate Psychopaths, especially the "organizational psychopath" subgroup (the group that manipulate their way into top management positions for the rewards and power that such positions confer and to take pleasure in the suffering and misery they cause to others along the way). His concern is that the benefits would be rather short-term, while the organizational harms may be longer lasting, granting that "organizational psychopaths" possess talents, such as persuasiveness, commitment to goal achievement, and creativity, which may make them "good producers" who enhance revenue generation. One of the cases that Clarke describes in *Working with Monsters* involves just such an individual, "Wayne," who was without doubt able to generate substantial revenue for the company he worked for (Wayne claimed to have doubled the company's revenue during his tenure there). However, along the way Wayne also managed to create massive turnover in the ranks of those he supervised (75% during one 18-month period) and create a dissatisfied client base due to his habit of making unfulfilled promises to them. In the short term, Wayne was a boon to the company he worked for, but that only lasted so long. As the evidence of his intraorganizational misdeeds began to mount and as his relations with his clients went south, the reputation of his employer also began to suffer. From a Customer Relations Management (CRM) perspective, Wayne had become an "organizational destroyer," as Boddy would label him. Given his lengthy experience consulting with organizations, Clarke is doubtful that if considered in the long-term there is any net benefit to be garnered from employing Corporate Psychopaths. Further support for the "long-term, net loss" position on the organizational benefits of Corporate Psychopaths can be found in a study by Wisniewski, Yekini, and Omar, which found that the "language characteristic of psychopaths present in annual report narratives, questionable integrity, excessive risk-taking and failure to contribute to charitable undertakings tend to reduce future shareholder wealth" (Wisniewski et al., 2017, p. 2).

CONCLUSION

In the previous chapter, we argued for the conclusion that, counterintuitive as it may sound, psychopathic personalities, in the form of Corporate Psychopaths and as job applicants, are likely covered under the Americans with Disabilities Act. "Psychopathy" would qualify as a "mental disorder." This would make the kind of psychopathy screening called for by the Corporate Psychopath Hypothesis illegal. In this chapter, we covered a set of ethical issues that arise for the use of pre-employment and post-hire psychopathy screening, issues that would remain even if the ADA were legislatively amended or interpreted by courts so as to not extend protection to psychopathic personalities. A basic concern for equal opportunity, a concern that would characterize a just society not just politically but economically as well, would be at risk in employment psychopathy screening due to the uncertainty that surrounds the reliability and predictive validity of those screening instruments that most likely would be used as part of the screening process. The potential for false positives would create scenarios where job applicants or employees were incorrectly identified as having psychopathic personalities and denied employment based on that incorrect diagnosis despite the fact that they may be entirely capable of performing the functions that are essential or even incidental to the job. We argued that psychopathy screening would constitute an intrusion into a job applicant's or employee's right to privacy given that we generally regard mental health information as information individuals have a right to keep private. Considered as a *prima facie* right, not an absolute one, the right to privacy can be justifiably intruded upon if certain conditions are met. Using a set of just such conditions as described by Persson and Hansson, we showed that the arguments for using psychopathy screening to prevent harmful and unjust treatment at the hands of Corporate Psychopaths and to protect the organization itself from the risky decision-making and behavior of Corporate Psychopaths would not satisfy the criteria set out by Persson and Hansson as necessary to justify intrusions into employee privacy. We finished this chapter by examining the merits of a general utilitarian approach to the question of employment psychopathy screening. Allowing, per Dutton, that the presence of Corporate Psychopaths, in the right situations, actually produces benefits for the organizations that employ them, we found lacking the argument that those benefits when weighed against the "costs" of employing psychopathic personalities would produce a "net gain" for organizations. Overall, unless other arguments for employment screening for psychopathy were to emerge, it seems unlikely that the practice could pass ethical muster.

Though the arguments presented here and in the previous chapter share a basic conclusion in common, namely that psychopathic personalities are deserving of protection (legal and ethical) against the use of employment screening aimed at uncovering their psychopathy, they do differ in one important way. The ethical arguments presented in this chapter contain as a premise the fact that there is absent a professional consensus regarding the reliability and validity of current psychopathy screening instruments. That premise matters because it is an essential part of the argument that psychopathy screening has the potential to deny some individuals equal opportunity and equal treatment, undermines part of an argument that employers are justified in invading the privacy of employees and job applicants, and diminishes the chance that a utilitarian argument could be mounted in defense of psychopathy screening. The arguments presented in this chapter are, for the most part, conditional arguments, their strength tied to the status of psychopathy tests like the PCL-R as reliable and valid psychological screens. The argument that psychopathic personalities can reasonably be considered to be covered by the protections and accommodations requirements set forth in the ADA is not a conditional argument in this sense. Apart from whether there exist any reliable and valid screening tools available for identifying and assessing the risk threat of psychopathic personalities, they are covered by the ADA because psychopathy fits the ADA definition of "disability." Future improvements in current psychopathy screening instruments or the development of better ones would not alter that general conclusion. If the reliability and validity issue could be resolved adequately, then the ethical arguments presented in this chapter, excluding those parts of the "violation of the right to privacy" argument that aren't necessarily tied to the reliability and validity issue (e.g., the sub-argument that the information employers would need to justify the termination of an employee with a psychopathic personality can be gained without the use of an intrusive means like a psychological screen) would lose their argumentative bite, as it were.

Conclusion

In the concluding section of *Corporate Psychopaths*, Boddy sums up the case against Corporate Psychopaths with a lengthy list of the dangers they pose.

> The research presented in this book suggests that Corporate Psychopaths are a major cause of organizational destruction in many ways. Modern organisations inadvertently look for them when hiring new employees and favour them in the selection procedures used. They gain promotion on the basis of a false persona, work they have not really done and success they have not really achieved. Their presence reduces job satisfaction among others and causes good employees to withdraw from organisations, thereby diluting the effectiveness of the human resource available to the organization. They create conflict and bullying out of all proportion to their small numbers. They use organizational rules to their own advantage and to control other employees, and they amplify any existing organizational constraints and thereby lower productivity. They reduce perceptions of corporate social responsibility and thus the attractiveness of organisations to ethical employees. They increase the workload of others by their parasitic and disruptive behavior in the workplace. (Boddy, 2011b, p. 174)

For Boddy, this is only the "tip of the iceberg" as he expects further research would show that the presence of Corporate Psychopaths also negatively impacts company longevity, levels of fraud, employee mental health, counterproductive work behavior, etc. (Boddy, 2011b, pp. 174–175).

Similarly, in the epilogue to his *Working with Monsters*, Clarke sounds the alarm for continued social ignorance of the presence of Corporate Psychopaths and the damage they cause.

> The second reason [for writing *Working with Monsters*] was to unravel the factors that make up the workplace psychopath in order to educate others about

> their potential danger. Society cannot afford to ignore workplace psychopaths, and it is only through greater understanding that we can begin to tackle the problem. Until we address our silent acceptance of the workplace psychopath, I believe we are to some extent complicit in their behaviours through our own inaction. After all, what difference, if any, exists between the person who tacitly condones the workplace psychopath's behavior and the workplace psychopath themselves? (Clarke, 2005, p. 284)

Though we might be inclined to reply that there is one critical difference between the "condoners" of workplace psychopaths' behavior and the workplace psychopaths themselves, namely that the "condoners" are not psychopathic personalities, the charge to organizations to become better at identifying and not harboring Corporate Psychopaths is a reasonable one to offer.

In this text, we have tried to present as robust a picture as possible of what we have referred to as the Corporate Psychopath Hypothesis. Along the way, we have tried to be as uncritical as possible of some of the defining empirical claims embedded in the hypothesis. It was not the intent of this work to conclusively judge the entire hypothesis, one way or the other. Instead, specific criticisms were introduced where they had importance for the focus of this work, namely the ethical and legal issues that would attend actual psychological screening of job applicants and current employees for psychopathy. We endeavored to work with as precise an understanding of "psychopathic personality" as possible so as to avoid having the arguments presented against employment screening for psychopathy cover cases where what is sought is information about only a small set of personality traits, such as egocentricity or superficial charm. Hiring for "culture fit" has become a much trumpeted, contemporary approach to recruitment and selection. Though the idea of hiring for "culture fit" introduces its own set of ethical concerns, for example the possibility that "culture fit" can be used as a cover for discriminatory hiring, an employer's interest in gauging the extent to which an applicant would function well as part of a team (their egocentricity dial is set at a low volume) or would excel in sales (their superficial charm dial is cranked up) are legitimate business interests that don't, immediately at least, raise any ethical red flags. What we have focused on is the call for screening for a purported, particular mental *disorder* itself, not the desire to screen for any particular trait or small subset of traits. The arguments presented herein are to be understood only in relation to that purpose.

There is an intuitive element to the Corporate Psychopath Hypothesis, one that accounts for its popular appeal over the past decade. Intentionally at times, popular media has portrayed corporate executives in ways that sound very similar to the description of Corporate Psychopaths. In the tradition of *Wall Street*, they are presented as greedy, uncaring, egotistical, ruthless in their business dealings, willing to break the law in pursuit of financial gain, etc. This social meme has come to dominate the public consciousness, and has for decades been used as the ground of political movements like Occupy Wall Street and of any number of political campaigns. We have, in effect, been conditioned to believe that corporate leaders, *as a group*, have a common character type, and one that puts them at odds with the economic pursuit of the common good. Against this backdrop, the introduction of the Corporate Psychopath Hypothesis makes sense intuitively. Our contemporary "social intuition" is that corporate leaders are in practice psychopathic personalities, even though we lacked the psychological label to use to capture that social sense. The Corporate Psychopath Hypothesis provided that language.

Boddy, Babiak, and Hare, and all the other researchers who have worked diligently over the past three decades to move the Corporate Psychopath Hypothesis beyond just an intuitive, anecdotally driven theory of corporate malfeasance are to be commended. The task they have taken on is not an easy one. The status of psychopathy as a valid psychological construct is something they have had to fight for, as many in the academic and clinical worlds have argued that it is not a distinct mental disorder unto itself. The "psychopathy is a thing" camp's dispute with the authors of the *DSM* is now in its seventh decade, with no sign that it may finally be resolved. They have had to constantly defend the scientific reliability and validity of the research instruments they employ as well as defend the view that the relatively small body of research findings they have been able to generate is representative of the demographic world the Corporate Psychopath Hypothesis covers. Sometimes successfully, sometimes unsuccessfully, defenders of the Corporate Psychopath Hypothesis have battled the tendency to use "psychopath" in loose ways for rhetorical or publishing purposes (e.g., to popularize their books). Yet, given the barriers to access they have faced in research efforts to conduct studies directly on senior-level managers and corporate executives, the demographic classes most often targeted in the Corporate Psychopath Hypothesis literature, they have been able to build in scientifically entrepreneurial ways a working body of research upon which to erect the scaffolding of the hypothesis.

That said, the speculative nature of the Corporate Psychopath Hypothesis must be acknowledged. Though there is much more empirical research present than there was when the hypothesis was first seriously floated nearly three decades ago, that research remains insufficient to the task of firmly establishing the core empirical claims contained in the Corporate Psychopath Hypothesis. As Smith and Lilienfeld noted in 2013, "The gap between popular coverage and scientific research on business psychopathy is both substantial and troubling" (Smith & Lilienfeld, 2013, p. 205). That gap remains.

For the Corporate Psychopath Hypothesis to remain of academic interest heading forward, it needs research bolstering on a number of points. First, and this is actually no fault of the proponents of the hypothesis, there needs to be the development of a body of psychopathy measurements of identifiable senior-level managers/executives, not just anecdotally-based, composite personalities or unidentified "managers I have worked for" that are the subject of much of the research data currently available. Gaining access to employees to screen for psychopathy has proven exceedingly difficult, and will likely continue to be so. As noted in chapter two, there is really only a trio of studies with any scale to them that involve psychopathy assessment of, though individually anonymous, an identifiable group of senior managers or executives. That data base needs to be increased significantly. Second, and relatedly, the development of a convincing body of empirical evidence for the unusually high rate of psychopathic personalities in higher levels of business organizations needs to involve the kind of screening used in the application of the PCL-R in criminal and clinical settings. That is, instead of self-report screening or screening based entirely on the responses of coworkers, the data gathering that would be most supportive of the Corporate Psychopath Hypothesis should involve the interview component of the PCL-R screen. Again, this would require direct, not mediated access to the individuals to be screened, something that has proven elusive. Since, if enacted, employment screening for psychopathy as part of the "seek and destroy" portion of the Corporate Psychopath Hypothesis would involve just such direct screening, it is only fair that the evidence cited as supporting the need to engage in such "seek and destroy" efforts be similarly focused. Third, the claim that Corporate Psychopaths potentially pose a number of serious risks to coworkers, the organizations that employ them, and the larger social/economic systems of which their home organizations are a part is beyond dispute. There is a robust research base showing that the core psychopathic personality traits, when exhibited in observable managerial behaviors, are strongly correlated with negative impacts on fellow employees and on the health of organizations themselves. What needs further empirical clarification is the nature of that risk. What is the real-world frequency with which identifiable Corporate Psychopaths engage in specific harm-causing behaviors? Of course, establishing this is dependent on more precisely identifying the presence of Corporate Psychopaths than has been done to this point. However, even if a more fine-grained map of the presence of Corporate Psychopaths can be established, if the construct "functioning/successful psychopaths" is meaningfully applicable to Corporate Psychopaths (which, as has been discussed earlier, it is argued tend to evade detection because they are able to "function well" in corporate settings), then an accurate and consistent means for measuring the actual risk they pose, similar to what goes in criminal sentencing processes, will need to be developed. As long as the normative, prescriptive part of the Corporate Psychopath Hypothesis is grounded in harm-based concerns, it is incumbent upon the defenders of the hypothesis to establish the seriousness of the risks involved. They cannot remain mostly speculative. Efforts to fill in these gaps in the current empirical research on Corporate Psychopaths will continue to be plagued by doubts about the reliability and validity of the measurement instruments used.

The impetus for this text was the lack of attention to the ethical issues that would attach to employment screening for psychopathy, not that the potential for such issues to arise has gone entirely unnoted. In passing at the end of *Corporate Psychopaths*, Boddy recognizes the potential for employment screening for psychopathy to violate a basic component of a just society.

> Corporate Psychopaths who have not overtly or identifiably acted on their ruthless impulses may come to be penalized if they are identified as such before they have acted unethically, immorally, ruthlessly or illegally. This raises ethical issues as to how Corporate Psychopaths should be treated, because acting in any way that biases their chances would seem to be contrary to the concept of natural justice and to the laws of some countries. (Boddy, 2011b, p. 173)

However, he then "shrugs off" such concerns by claiming that "passive" monitoring of the activities of suspected Corporate Psychopaths would likely not violate any justice principles. To be clear, the argument presented here *is not* that it would be unethical for Corporate Psychopaths to be removed from the workplace when they cause harm to others or the organization itself. As for any employee, when Corporate Psychopaths behave in unacceptable ways, employers have the right to terminate them. The argument *has* been that the use of employment screening for psychopathy as the first step in doing so is likely illegal and unethical. The argument is, in a way, only a limited defense of Corporate Psychopaths.

Bibliography

ADA. 1990. United States Department of Justice, Civil Rights Division. https://www.ada.gov/2010_regs.htm.

American Psychiatric Association. 1980. *Diagnostic and Statistical Manual of Mental Disorders* (3rd edition). Washington, D.C.: American Psychiatric Association.

American Psychiatric Association. 2013. *Diagnostic and Statistical Manual of Mental Disorders* (DSM-5). Washington, D.C.

Andersson, L. M., and Pearson, C. M. 1999. "Tit for Tat? The Spiraling Effect of Incivility in the Workplace." *Academy of Management Review, 24*: 452–471.

Andrews, H. 2015. "Psychopathic Traits and Career Interests—What Do Psychopathic Undergraduates Study and What Do They Want to Do?" *EAWOP Congress: Respectful and Effective Leadership. Managing People and Organisations in Turbulent Times*. European Association of Work and Organisational Psychology, Oslo.

Ariely, D. 2012. *The Honest Truth about Dishonesty: How We Lie to Everyone—Especially Ourselves*. New York: HarperCollins.

Arrigo, B. A. and Shipley, S. 2001. "The Confusion over Psychopath (i): Historical Considerations." *International Journal of Offender Therapy and Comparative Criminology, 45*(3): 325–344.

Babiak, P. 1995. "When Psychopaths Go to Work: A Case Study of an Industrial Psychopath." *Applied Psychology: An International Review, 44*: 171–188.

Babiak, P. 2000. "Psychopathic Manipulation at Work." In C. B. Gacono (ed.), *The Clinical and Forensic Assessment of Psychopathy: A Practitioner's Guide* (pp. 287–311). Mahwah, NJ: Erlbaum.

Babiak, P. and Hare, R. D. 2006. *Snakes in Suits: When Psychopaths Go to Work*. New York: HarperCollins.

Babiak, P., Neumann, C.S., and Hare, R.D. 2010. "Corporate psychopathy: Talking the Walk." *Behavioral Sciences & the Law*, 28(2): 174–193.

Bartels, D. M. and Pizarro, D. A. 2011. "The Mismeasure of Morals: Antisocial Traits Predict Utilitarian Responses to Moral Dilemmas." *Cognition, 121*: 154–161.

Baskin-Sommers, A., Stuppy-Sullivan, A. M., and Buckholts, J. W. 2016. "Psychopathic Individuals Exhibit but Do Not Avoid Regret during Counterfactual Decision Making." *Proceedings of the National Academy of Sciences, 113*(50): 14438–14443.

Bate, C., Boduszek, D., Dhingra, K., and Bale, C. 2014. "Psychopathy, Intelligence, and Emotional Responding in a Non-Forensic Sample: An Experimental Investigation." *The Journal of Forensic Psychiatry & Psychology, 25*(5): 600–612.

Baumeister, R. F., Vohs, K. D., and Tice, D. M. 2007. "The Strength Model of Self-Control." *Current Directions in Psychological Science, 16*: 351–355.

Birbaumer, N., Veit, R., Lotze, M., Erb, M., Hermann, C., Grodd, W., and Flor, H. 2005. "Deficient Fear Conditioning in Psychopathy: A Functional Magnetic Resonance Imaging Study." *Archives of General Psychiatry, 62*(7): 799–805.

Blair, R. J. R. 2013. "Psychopathy: Congitive and Neural Dysfunction." *Dialogues in Clinical Neuroscience, 15*(2); 181–190.

Board, B. J. and Fritzon, K. 2005. "Disordered Personalities at Work." *Psychology, Crime & Law, 11*(1): 17–32.

Boddy, C. R. 2005. "The Implications of Corporate Psychopathy for Business and Society: An Initial Examination and A Call to Arms." *Australasian Journal of Business and Behavioral Sciences, 1*(2): 30–40.

Boddy, C. R. 2006. "The Dark Side of Management Decisions: Organizational Psychopaths." *Management Decision, 44*(10): 1461–1475.

Boddy, C. R. 2010. "Corporate Psychopaths and Organizational Types." *Journal of Public Affairs, 10*: 300–312.

Boddy, C. R. 2011a. "Corporate Psychopaths, Bullying, and Unfair Supervision in the Workplace." *Journal of Business Ethics, 100:* 367–379.

Boddy, C. R. 2011b. *Corporate psychopaths: Organizational destroyers*. New York: Palgrave MacMillan.

Boddy, C. R. 2011c. "The Corporate Psychopaths Theory of the Global Financial Crisis." *Journal of Business Ethics, 102:* 255–259.

Boddy, C. R. 2014. "Corporate Psychopaths, Conflict, Employee Affective Well-Being and Counterproductive Work Behavior." *Journal of Business Ethics, 121:* 107–121.

Boddy, C. R. 2015a. "Organizational Psychopaths: A Ten-Year Update." *Management Decision, 53*(10): 2407–2432.

Boddy, C. R. 2015b. "Psychopathic Leadership: A Case Study of a Corporate Psychopath CEO." *Journal of Business Ethics*, 145: 141–156.

Boddy, C. R., Ladyshewsky, R., and Galvin, P. 2010a. "Leaders Without Ethics in Global Business: Corporate Psychopaths." *Journal of Public Affairs, 10:* 121–138.

Boddy, C. R., Ladyshewsky, R., and Galvin, P. 2010b. "The Influence of Corporate Psychopaths on Corporate Social Responsibility and Organizational Commitment to Employees." *Journal of Business Ethics, 97:* 1–19.

Boddy, C. R., Miles, D., Chandana, S., and Hartog, M. 2015. "Extreme Managers, Extreme Workplace: Capitalism, Organizations, and Corporate Psychopaths." *Organization, 22*(4): 530–551.

Brazil, I. A., and Cima, M. 2016. "Contemporary Approaches to Psychopathy." In Maaike Cima (ed.), *The Handbook of Forensic Psychopathology and Treatment*, New York, NY: Routledge: 206–226.

Bruk-Lee, V., and Spector, P. E. 2006. "The Social Stressors–Counterproductive Work Behaviors Link: Are Conflicts with Supervisors and Coworkers the Same?" *Journal of Occupational Health Psychology, 11*(2): 145–156.

Cavico, F. J., Mujtaba, B. G., Lawrence, E., and Muffler, S. C. 2015. "Personality Tests in Employment: A Continuing Legal, Ethical, and Practical Quandary." *Advances in Social Sciences Research Journal, 2*(3): 60–84.

Clarke, J. 2005. *Working with Monsters: How to Identify and Protect Yourself from the Workplace Psychopath*. Sydney: Random House.

Clarke, J. 2007. *The Pocket Psycho*. Sydney: Random House.

Cleckley, H. 1941. *The Mask of Sanity: An Attempt to Reinterpret Some Issues About the Co-Called Psychopathic Personality*. St. Louis, Missouri: Mosby.

Cohan, W. D. 2012a. "Did Psychopaths Take Over Wall Street Asylum?" Bloomberg Businessweek. www.bloomberg.com/opinion/articles/2012-01-03/did-psychopaths-take-over-wall-street-asylum-commentary-by-william-cohan.

Cohan, W. D. 2012b. "This is How Wall Street Psychopaths Caused the Financial Crisis." https://www.businessinsider.com/bill-cohan-an-academic-describes-how-wall-street-psychopaths-caused-the-financial-crisis-2012-1.

Cooke, D. J., Hart, S. D., and Michie, C. 2004. "Cross-national Differences in the Assessment of Psychopathy: Do They Reflect Variations in Raters' Perceptions of Symptoms?" *Psychological Assessment, 16*, 335–339.

Crego, C., and Widiger, T. A. 2015. "Psychopathy and the DSM." *Journal of Personality, 83*(6): 665–677.

Davis, O. June 23, 2017. "Don't Give Your Money to Psychopaths, says science." *CNBC*. www.cnbc.com/2017/06/23/dont-give-your-money-to-psychopaths-says-science.html.

Decety, J., Chen, C., Harenski, C., and Kiehl, K. 2013. "An fMRI Study of Affective Perspective Taking in Individuals with Psychopathy: Imaging Others in Pain Does Not Evoke Empathy." *Frontiers in Human Neuroscience*. DOI: 10.3389/fnhum.2013.00489.

DeMatteo, D., Edens, J. F., Galloway, M., Cox, J., Smith, S. T., and Formon, D. 2014. "The Role and Reliability of the Psychopathy Checklist Revised in U.S. Sexually Violent Predator Evaluations: A Case Law Survey." *Law and Human Behavior, 38*, 248–255.

Desjardins, J., and Duska, R. 2005. "Drug Testing in Employment." In Joseph R. Desjardins & John J. McCall (eds.), *Contemporary issues in business ethics*, 4th edition. Belmont, CA: Wadsworth: 222–227.

Donaldson, T. and Dunfee, T. W. 1999. *The Ties that Bind: A Social Contracts Approach to Business Ethics*. Boston: Harvard Business School Press.

Dutton, K. 2012. *The Wisdom of Psychopaths: What Saints, Spies, and Serial Killers Can Teach Us About Success*. Kindle ed. New York: Scientific American/ Farrar, Straus & Giroux.

Edens, J. F., Marcus, D. K., Lilienfeld, S. O., and Polythress, N.G. 2006. "Psychopathic, Not Psychopath: Taxometric Evidence for the Dimensional Structure of Psychopathy." *Journal of Abnormal Psychology, 115*, 131–144.

Edens, J. F., Cox, J., Smith, S. T., DeMatteo, D., and Sörman, K. 2015. "How Reliable are Psychopathy Checklist Revised Scores in Canadian Criminal Trials? A Case Law Review." A case law review. *Psychological Assessment, 27*, 447–456.

Equal Employment Opportunity Commission. (1992). "Technical Assistance Manual for Title I of the Americans with Disabilities Act." EEOC-M-1A.

Equal Employment Opportunity Commission. (1997). "EEOC Enforcement Guidance on the Americans with Disabilities Act and Psychiatric Disabilities." EEOC 915.002.

U.S. Equal Employment Opportunity Commission. 2007. *EEOC Fact Sheet on Employment Tests and Selection Procedures.* https://www.eeoc.gov/laws/guidance/employment-tests-and-selection-procedures.

Flor, H., Birbaumer, N., Hermann, C., Ziegler, S., and Patrick, C. J. 2002. "Aversive Pavlovian Conditioning in Psychopaths: Peripheral and Central Correlates." *Psychophysiology, 39*(4): 505–518.

Folger, R., and Skarlicki, D. P. 1998. "A Popcorn Metaphor for Employee Aggression." In R. Griffin, A. O'Leary-Kelly, & J. Collins (Eds.), *Dysfunctional behavior in organizations: Violent and deviant behavior* (pp. 43–81). Stamford, CT: JAI Press.

Fowler, K. A. and Lilienfeld, S. O. 2007. "The Psychopathy q-sort: Construct Validity Evidence in a Nonclinical Sample." *Assessment, 14*(1): 75–79.

French, P. A. 1979. "The Corporation as a Moral Person." *American Philosophical Quarterly, 16:* 207–215.

Frydman, C., Camerer, C., Bossaerts, P., and Rangel, A. 2011. MAOA-L carriers are better at making optimal financial decisions under risk. *Proceedings of the Royal Society B, 278*(1714): 2053–2059.

Gacono, C. B., and Hutton, H. E. 1994. "Suggestions for the Clinical and Forensic Use of the Hare Psychology Checklist-Revised (PCL-R)." *International Journal of Law and Psychiatry, 17*, 303–317.

Gao, Y. and Tang, S. 2013. "Psychopathic Personality and Utilitarian Moral Judgment in College Students." *Journal of Criminal Justice, 41*, 342–349.

Goodstein, L. D., and Lanyon, R. I. "Applications of Personality Assessment to the Workplace: A Review." *Journal of Business and Psychology, 13*(3): 291–322.

Grann, M., Långström, N., Tengström, A., and Stålenheim, E. G. 1998. "Reliability of File-Based Retrospective Ratings of Psychopathy with the PCL-R." *Journal of Personality Assessment, 70*, 416–426.

Gregory, S., Blair, R. J., Fytche, D., Simmons, A., Kumari, V., Hodgins, S., and Blackwood, N. 2015. "Punishment and Psychopathy: A Case-control Functional MRI Investigation of Reinforcement Learning in Violent Antisocial Personality Disordered Men." *The Lancet Psychiatry, 2*(2): 153–160.

Guay, J. P., Ruscio, J., Knight, R. A., and Hare, R. D. 2007. "A Taxometric Analysis of the Latent Structure of Psychopathy: Evidence for Dimensionality." *Journal of Abnormal Psychology, 116*, 701–716.

Hamilton, R. B., and Newman, J. P. 2018. “The Response Modulation Hypothesis: For Mulation, Development, and Implications.” In Christopher J. Patrick (ed.), *Handbook of Psychopathy*, 2nd edition, New York, NY: The Guilford Press: (pp. 80–93).

Han, G. H., Harms, P. D., and Bai, Y. 2017. “Nightmare Bosses: The Impact of Abusive Supervision on Employees’ Sleep, Emotions, and Creativity.” *Journal of Business Ethics, 145:* 21–31.

Hare, R. D. 1970. *Psychopathy: Theory and Research*. New York: Wiley.

Hare, R. D. 1986. “Twenty Years of Experience with the Cleckley Psychopath.” In W. H. Reid, D. Dorr, J. I. Walker, and J. W. Bonner III, (eds.). *Unmasking the Psychopath* (pp. 3–27). New York: Norton.

Hare, R. D. 1999. *Without Conscience: The Disturbing World of the Psychopaths Among Us.* New York: Guilford Press.

Hare, R. D. 2003. *The Hare Psychopathy Checklist Revised.* Toronto, Ontario, Canada: Multi-Health Systems.

Hare, R. D., Clark, D., Grann, M., and Thornton, D. 2000. “Psychopathy and the Predictive Validity of the PCL-R: An International Perspective.” *Behavioral Sciences and the Law*, 18(5): 623-645.

Harris, G. T., Skilling, T. A., and Rice, M. E. 2001. “The Construct of Psychopathy.” In M. Tonry & N. Morris (eds). *Crime and Justice: An Annual Review of Research*, (pp. 197–264). Chicago: University of Chicago Press.

Hartley, D. Sept. 23, 2016. “5 Ways of the Corporate Psychopath.” *Psychology Today*. www.psychologytoday.com/us/blog/machiavellians-gulling-the-rubes/201609/5-ways-the-corporate-psychopath.

Harris, G. T. and Rice, M. E. 2006. “Treatment of Psychopathy: A Review of Empirical Findings.” In C. J. Patrick (ed.), *Handbook of Psychopathy* (pp. 555–572). New York: Guilford Press.

Harris, G. T., Rice, M. E., and Cormier, C. A. 1991. “Psychopathy and Violent Recidivism.” *Law and Human Behavior, 15*(6), 625–637.

Hauge, L. J., Skogstad, A., and Einarsen, S. 2009. “Individual and Situational Predictors of Workplace Bullying: Why Do Perpetrators Engage in the Bullying of Others?” *Work & Stress, 23*(4): 349–358.

Hawes, S. W., Boccaccini, M. T., and Murrie, D. C. 2013. “Psychopathy and the Combination of Psychopathy and Sexual Deviance as Predictors of Sexual Recidivism: Meta-Analytic Findings the Psychopathy Checklist–Revised.” *Psychological Assessment, 25*, 233–243.

Henderson, D. K. 1939. *Psychopathic States*. New York: W. W. Norton & Co.

Hoppenbrouwers, S. S., Bulten, B. H., and Brazil, I. A. 2016. “Parsing Fear: A Reassessment of the Evidence for Fear Deficits in Psychology.” *Psychological Bulletin, 142*(6): 573–600.

Hough, L. H., Eaton, N. K., Dunnette, M. D., Kamp, J. D., and McCloy, R. A. 1990. “Criterion-related Validities of Personality Constructs and the Effects of Response Distortions on these Validities.” *Journal of Applied Psychology, 75*(5): 581–595.

Hurst, C., Simon, L., Jung, Y., and Pirouz, D. 2019. “Are ‘Bad’ Employees Happier under Bad Bosses? Differing Effects of Abusive Supervision on Low and High Primary Psychopathy Employees.” *Journal of Business Ethics, 158:* 1149–1164.

Jeandarme, I., Edens, J., Habets, P., Bruckers, L., Oei, K., and Bogaerts, S. 2017. "PCL-R Field Validity in Prison and Hospital Settings." *Law and Human Behavior, 41*(1): 29–43.

Jeppesen, K. K. and Leder, C. 2016. "Auditors' Experience with Corporate Psychopaths." *Journal of Financial Crime, 23*(4): 870–881.

Jonason, P. K., Li, N. P., Buss, D. M. 2010. "The Costs and Benefits of the Dark Triad: Implications for Mate Poaching and Mate Retention Tactics." *Personality and Individual Differences, 48:* 373–378.

Jonason, P. K., Li, N. P., Webster, G. W., and Schmitt, D. R. 2009. "The Dark Triad: Facilitating a Short-Term Mating Strategy in Men." *European Journal of Personality, 23:* 5–18.

Jones, D. N. and Hare, R. D. 2016. "The Mismeasure of Psychopathy: A Commentary on Boddy's PM-MRV." *Journal of Business Ethics, 138:* 579–588.

Jurjako, M. 2019. "Is Psychopathy a Harmful Dysfunction?" *Biology & Philosophy, 34*(5): 1–23.

Kahn, W. 1998. "Relational Systems at Work." In Staw, B., Cumming, L.L. (eds.), *Research in Organizational Behavior, Vol. 20. An Annual Series of Analytical Essays and Critical Reviews*, Greenwich, Connecticut: JAI Press: 39–76.

Karraker v. Rent-A-Center, Inc. 2005. https://caselaw.findlaw.com/us-7th-circuit/1486883.html.

Kets de Vries, M. F. R. and Miller, D. 1984. *The Neurotic Organization: Diagnosing and Changing Counterproductive Styles of Management.* San Francisco: Jossey-Bass.

Kets de Vries, M. F. R. and Miller, D. 2005. "Narcissim and Leadership. An Object Relations Perspective." *Human Relations, 38:* 583–601.

Kiehl, K. A., Smith, A. M., Hare, R. D., Mendrek, A., Forster, B. B., Brink, J., and Liddle, P. F. 2001. "Limbic Abnormalities in Affective Processing by Criminal Psychopaths as Revealed by Functional Magnetic Resonance Imaging." *Biological Psychiatry, 50*(9): 677–684.

Kiehl, K. A., and Hoffman, M. B. 2011. "The Criminal Psychopath: History, Neuroscience, Treatment, and Economics." *Jurimetrics, 51:* 355–397.

Koch, J. L. A. 1888. *Kurzgefaßter Leitfaden der Psychiatrie* (Short Textbook of Psychiatry).

Koch, J. L. A. 1891–1893. *Die psychopathischen Minderwertigkeiten* (Psychopathic Inferiority).

Kohll, A. January 31, 2018. "5 Reasons Social Connections Can Enhance Your Employee Wellness Program." *Forbes Magazine*. https://www.forbes.com/sites/alankohll/2018/1/31/5-ways-social-connections-can-enhance-your-employee-wellness-program/#46069309527c.

Krupp, D. B., Sewall, L. A., Lalumière, M. L., Sheriff, C., and Harris, G. T. 2013. "Psychopathy, Adaptation, and Disorder." *Frontiers in Psychology, 4:*1–5.

Lapierre, L. M., Spector, P. E., and Leck, J. D. 2005. "Sexual versus Nonsexual Workplace Aggression and Victims' Overall Job Satisfaction: A Meta-Analysis." *Journal of Occupational Health Psychology, 10*(2): 155–169.

Lee, R. T., and Brotheridge, C. M. 2006. "When Prey Turns Predatory: Workplace Bullying as a Predictor of Counteraggression/Bullying, Coping, and Well-Being." *European Journal of Work and Organizational Psychology, 5:* 165–184.

Leistedt, S. J. and Linkowski, P. 2014. "Psychopathy and the Cinema: Fact or Fiction?" *Journal of Forensic Science, 59*(1): 167–174.

Lewis, D. O. 2017. "Adult Antisocial Behavior, Criminality, and Violence." In B. Sadock, V. Sadock, and P. Ruiz (eds.), *Kaplan and Sadock's Comprehensive Textbook of Psychiatry, 10th edition*, South Holland, Netherlands: Wolters and Kluwer, (pp. 2413–2430).

Leymann, H. 1996. "The Content and Development of Mobbing at Work." *European Journal of Work and Organizational Psychology, 5*(2), 165–184.

Lloyd, C. D., Clark, H. J., and Forth, A. E. 2010. "Psychopathy, Expert Testimony, and Indeterminate Sentences: Exploring the Relationship between Psychopathy Checklist–Revised Testimony and Trial Outcome in Canada." *Legal and Criminological Psychology, 15*: 323–339.

Lykken, D. T. 1957. "A Study of Anxiety in the Sociopathic Personality." *The Journal of Abnormal and Social Psychology, 55*: 6–10.

Lykken, D. T. 1995. *The Antisocial Personalities.* Hillsdale, NJ: Lawrence Erlbaum Associates.

Machan, T. R. 1987. "Human Rights, Workers' Rights, and the 'Right' to Occupational Safety." In G. Ezorsky (ed.), *Moral Rights in the Workplace*. Albany: State University of New York Press.

Magee, C., Gordon, R., Robinson, L., Caputi, P., and Oades, L. 2017. "Workplace Bullying and Absenteeism: The Mediating Roles of Poor Health and Work Engagement." *Human Resource Management Journal, 27*(3): 319-334.

Mahaffey, K. J. and Marcus, D. K. 2006. "Interpersonal Perception of Psychopathy: A Social Relations Analysis." *Journal of Social and Clinical Psychology, 25*(1): 53–74.

Marshall, A. J., Ashleigh, M., Baden, D., Ojiako, U., and Guidi, M. G. D. 2014. "Corporate Psychopathy: Can 'Search and Destroy' and "Hearts and Minds' Military Metaphors Inspire HRM Solutions?" *Journal of Business Ethics, 128*(3): 495–504.

Martin, A. and Matiaske, W. 2017. "Absenteeism as a Reaction to Harmful Behavior in the Workplace from a Stress Theory Point of View." *Management Revue, 28*(2): 227–254.

Martens, W. H. J. 2008. "The Problem with Robert Hare's Psychopathy Checklist: Incorrect Conclusions, High Risk of Misuse, and Lack of Reliability." *Medicine and Law*, 27: 449–462.

Mathieu, C., Hare, R. D., Jones, D. N., Babiak, P., and Neumann, C. 2013. "Factor Structure of the B-Scan 360: A Measure of Corporate Psychopathy." *Psychological Assessment, 25*(1): 288–293.

May, L. 1983. "Vicarious Agency and Corporate Moral Agency." *Philosophical Studies, 43*: 69–82.

McAllister, C. P., and Perrewe, P. L. 2018. "About to Burst: How Self-Regulation Affects the Enactment of Bullying Behavior." *Journal of Business Ethics, 153*: 877–888.

Međedović, J., Petrović, B., Želeskov-Đorić, J., and Savić, M. 2017. "Interpersonal and Affective Psychopathy Traits can Enhance Human Fitness." *Evolutionary Psychological Science, 3*(4): 306–315.

Meloy, J. R., Book, A., Hosker-Field, A., Methot-Jones, T., and Roters, J. 2018. "Social, Sexual, and Violent Predation: Are Psychopathic Traits Evolutionarily Adaptive?" *Violence Gend* 5:153–165

Murrie, D. C., Boccaccini, M. T., Turner, D. B., Meeks, M., Woods, C., and Tussey, C. 2009. "Rater (dis)Agreement on Risk Assessment Measures in Sexually Violent Predator Proceedings: Evidence of Adversarial Allegiance in Forensic Evaluation?" *Psychology, Public Policy, and Law, 15:* 19–53.

Nathanson, C., Williams, K. M., and Paulhus, D. L. 2006. "Predictors of a Behavioral Measure of Scholastic Cheating: Personality and Competence but not Demographics." *Contemporary Educational Psychology, 31:* 97–122.

Neal, T., Miller, S. L., and Shealy, R. C. 2015. "A Field Study of a Comprehensive Violence Risk Assessment Battery." *Criminal Justice and Behavior, 42:* 952–968.

Neumann, C. S., Schmitt, D. S., Carter, R., Embley, I., and Hare, R. D. 2012. "Psychopathic Traits in Females and Males Across the Globe." *Behavioral Sciences and the Law, 30*(5): 557–574.

Nielsen, M. B. and Einarsen, S. V. 2102. "Outcomes of Exposure to Workplace Bullying: A Meta-Analytic Review." *Work & Stress, 26*(4): 309–332.

Nielsen, M. B. and Einarsen, S. V. 2018. "What We Know, What We Do Not Know, and What We Should and Could Have Known About Workplace Bullying: An Overview of the Literature and Agenda for Future Research." *Aggression and Violent Behavior, 42:* 71–83.

Osumi, T., and Ohiri, H. 2010. "The Positive Side of Psychopathy: Emotional Detachment in Psychopathy and Rational Decision-making in the Ultimatum Game." *Personality and Individual Differences, 49*(5): 451–456.

Patrick, C. J. (ed.). 2018. *Handbook of Psychopathy, 2nd edition.* New York: Guilford Press.

Pech, R. J. and Slade, B. W. 2007. "Organization Sociopaths: Rarely Challenged, Often Promoted. Why?" *Society and Business Review, 2*(3): 254–269.

Person, E. S. 1986. "Manipulativeness in Entrepreneurs and Psychopaths." In W. H. Reid, D. Dorr, J. I. Walker, and J. W. Bonner (eds.), *Unmasking the Psychopath: Antisocial Personality and Related Syndromes.* (pp. 256–274). New York: Norton.

Persson, A. J. and Hansson, S. O. 2003. "Privacy at Work–Ethical Criteria." *Journal of Business Ethics, 42:* 59–70.

Prichard, J. C. 1835. *A Treatise on Insanity and Other Disorders Affecting the Mind.* London: Sherwood, Gilbert, & Piper.

Quinn, D. P. and Jones, T. M. 1995. "An Agent Morality View of Business Policy." *Academy of Management Review, 20*(1): 22–42.

Rawls, J. 1999. *A Theory of Justice, revised edition.* Cambridge, Massachusetts: Belknap Press of Harvard University Press.

Reimer, M. 2008. "Psychopathy Without (the Language of) Disorder." *Neuroethics, 1:* 185–198.

Reuell, P. Feb. 2, 2017. "A Revised Portrait of Psychopaths." *Harvard Gazette*. https://news.harvard.edu/gazette/story/2017/02/a-revised-portrait-of-psychopaths/.

Rice, M. Harris, G., and Cormier, C. 1992. "An Evaluation of a Maximum Security Therapeutic Community for Psychopaths and Other Mentally Disordered Offenders." *Law and Human Behavior, 16:* 399–412.

Ritholtz, B. 2012. "Psychopaths Caused the Financial Crisis . . . And They Will Do It Again and Again Unless They are Removed from Power." https://ritholtz.com/2012/01/psychopaths-caused-the-financial-crisis/.

Robinson, S. L., and O'Leary-Kelly, A. M. 1998. "Monkey See, Monkey Do: The Influence of Work Groups on the Antisocial Behavior of Employees." *Academy of Management Journal, 41:* 658–672.

Rogers, T., Blackwood, N., Farnham, F., Pickup, G., and Watts, M. (2008). "Fitness to Plead and Competence to Stand Trial: A Systematic Review of the Construct and Its Application." *Journal of Forensic Psychiatry and Psychology, 19:* 576–596.

Sandberg, A. 2014. "Hiring the Right Psychopath." *Practical Ethics: Ethics in the news*. http://blog.practicalethics.ox.ac.uk/2014/09/hiring-the-right-psychopath/#more-9248.

Sepälä, E., and Cameron, K. December 1, 2015. "Proof that Positive Work Cultures are More Productive." *Harvard Business Review*. https://hbr.org/2015/12/proof-that-positive-work-cultures-are-more-productive.

Shiv, B., Loewenstein, G., and Bechara, A. 2005. "The Dark Side of Emotion in Decision-making: When Individuals with Decreased Emotional Reactions Make More Advantageous Decisions." *Cognitive Brain Research, 23*(1): 85–92.

Siegel, R. A. 1978. "Probability of Punishment and Suppression of Behavior in Psychopathic and Nonpsychopathic Offenders." *Journal of Abnormal Psychology, 87*(5): 514–522.

Singh, J. 2008. "Imposters Masquerading as Leaders: Can the Contagion be Contained?" *Journal of Business Ethic, 82*(3): 733–745.

Skeem, J. L., Monahan, J., and Mulvery, E. P. 2002. "Psychopathy, Treatment Involvement, and Subsequent Violence Among Civil Psychiatric Patients." *Law and Human Behavior, 26*(6): 577–603.

Smith, S. F., and Lilienfeld, S. O. 2013. "Psychopathy in the Workplace: The Knowns and Unknowns." *Aggression and Violent Behavior, 18:* 204–218.

Spindel, P. 2008. "How Not to Hire a Bully." *Canadian HR Reporter, 21:* 26.

Stringer, L. 2006. "The Link Between the Quality of the Supervisor Employee Relationship and the Level of the Employee's Job Satisfaction." *Public Organization Review, 6*(2): 125–142.

Tepper, B. J. 2000. "Consequences of Abusive Supervision." *Academy of Management Journal, 43*(2): 178–190.

Tiihonen, J., Vaurio, O., Laakso, M., Repo, E., Soininen, H., Aronen, H. J., Nieminen, H., and Savolainen, L. 2000. "Amygdaloid Volume Loss in Psychopathy." *Society for Neuroscience Abstracts, 26:* 1–2.

Tuttle, B. July 19, 2010. "Is Your Boss a Psychopath? Or Merely Mean." *Time Magazine*. www.business.time.com/2010/07/19/is-your-boss-a-psychopath-or-merely-mean.

Van den Brande, W., Baillien, E., De Witte, H., Elst, T. V., and Godderis, L. 2016. “The Role of Work Stressors, Coping Strategies, and Coping Resources in the Process of Workplace Bullying: A Systematic Review and Development of a Comprehensive Model.” *Aggression & Violent Behavior, 29:* 61–71.

Vitacco, M. J., Neumann, C. S., and Jackson, R. L. 2005. “Testing a Four-Factor Model of Psychopathy and Its Association with Ethnicity, Gender, Intelligence, and Violence.” *Journal of Consulting and Clinical Psychology, 73*(3): 466–476.

Voight, K. Jan. 20, 2012. “Bad Bosses: The Psycho-path to Success?” *CNN*. www.cnn.com/2102/01/19/business/psychopath-boss/index.html.

Wakefield, J. C. 1992. “The Concept of Mental Disorder: On the Boundary between Biological Facts and Social Values.” *American Psychologist, 47*(3): 373–388.

Widiger, T. A., Cadoret, R., Hare, R. D., Robins, L., Rutherford, M., Zanarini, M., Alterman, A., Apple, M., Corbitt, E., Forth, A., Hart, S., Kultermann, J., Woody, G., and Frances, A. 1996. “DSM-IV Antisocial Personality Disorder Field Trial.” *Journal of Abnormal Psychology, 105*(1): 3–16.

Willner, K. M., Sonrienberg, S. P., Wemmer, T. H., and Kochuba, M. 2016. “Workplace Personality Testing: Towards a Better Way of Determining Whether Personality Tests are Prohibted Pre-offer Medical Exams under the Americans with Disabilities Act.” *Employee Relations Law Journal, 42*(3): 4–27.

Wisniewski, T. P., Yekini, L. S., and Omar, A. Aug. 25, 2017. “Beware the Corporate Psychopath.” *Governance & Compliance*. www.icsa.org.uk/knowledge/governance-and-compliance/features/beware-the-corporate-psychopath.

Wisniewski, T. P., Yekini, L. S., & Omar, A. M. A. 2017. “Psychopathic Traits of Corporate Leadership as Predictors of Future Stock Returns.” https://papers.ssrn.com/sol3/papers.cfm?abstract_id=2984999

World Health Organization. 2018. *International Classification of Diseases and Related Health Problems*. www.who.int/health-topics/international-classification-of-diseases.

Index

About the Author

Brian K. Steverson is the John L. Aram Chair in Business Ethics in the School of Business Administration at Gonzaga University.

www.ingramcontent.com/pod-product-compliance
Ingram Content Group UK Ltd.
Pitfield, Milton Keynes, MK11 3LW, UK
UKHW012119150926
475560UK00002B/183

9 781793 616821